SEMINAR STUDIES IN HISTORY

General Editor: Roger Lockyer

Henry VII

Second Edition

Roger Lockyer

Senior Lecturer in History,
Royal Holloway College,
University of London

LONGMAN
London and New York

LONGMAN GROUP LIMITED,
*Longman House, Burnt Mill, Harlow, Essex CM20 2JE, England
and Associated Companies throughout the world.*

Published in the United States of America
by Longman Inc., New York

© Longman Group Limited 1968, 1983
*All rights reserved, no part of this publication
may be reproduced, stored in a retrieval system,
or transmitted in any form or by any means, electronic,
mechanical, photocopying, recording, or otherwise,
without the prior written permission of the Publishers.*

First published 1968
Second edition 1983
Second impression 1984
ISBN 0 582 35410 2

Set in 10/11pt Linotron Baskerville

*Printed in Malaysia
by Art Printing Works Sdn. Bhd., Kuala Lumpur.*

British Library Cataloguing in Publication Data

Lockyer, Roger
    Henry VII. – 2nd ed. – (Seminar studies series)
    1. Great Britain – History – Henry VII, 1485–1509
    I. Title   II. Series
    942.5'1   DA330
    ISBN 0-582-35410-2

Library of Congress Cataloging in Publication Data

Lockyer, Roger.
    Henry VII.
    (Seminar studies in history)
    Bibliography: p.
    Includes index.
    1. Great Britain – Politics and government – 1485–1509.
2. Finance, Public – Great Britain – To 1688. 3. Great Britain –
History – Henry VII, 1485–1509. I. Title. II. Series.
JN183 1485.L62 1983   942.05'1   82-23992
ISBN 0-582-35410-2 (pbk.)

Contents

Seminar Studies in History

Founding Editor: Patrick Richardson

Introduction

The Seminar Studies series was conceived by Patrick Richardson, whose experience of teaching history persuaded him of the need for something more substantial than a textbook chapter but less formidable than the specialised full-length academic work. He was also convinced that such studies, although limited in length, should provide an up-to-date and authoritative introduction to the topic under discussion as well as a selection of relevant documents and a comprehensive bibliography.

Patrick Richardson died in 1979, but by that time the Seminar Studies series was firmly established, and it continues to fulfil the role he intended for it. This book, like others in the series, is therefore a living tribute to a gifted and original teacher.

Note on the System of References:
A bold number in round brackets (**5**) in the text refers the reader to the corresponding entry in the Bibliography section at the end of the book. A bold number in square brackets, preceded by 'doc' [**doc. 6**] refers the reader to the corresponding items in the section of Documents, which follows the main text.

ROGER LOCKYER
General Editor

Acknowledgements

We are indebted to the following for permission to reproduce copyright material:

Connecticut State Library for extracts from the article 'Lord Hastings' Indentured Retainers 1461–1483: The Lawfulness of Livery and Retaining under the Yorkists and Tudors' by W.N. Dunham Jnr. *Transactions of the Connecticut Academy of Arts & Sciences*, Vol 39, pub. Yale University Press 1955; The Controller of Her Majesty's Stationery Office for extracts from *Calender of the Close Rolls* Henry VII, Vol 1 1485–1500, & Vol II 1500–1509, pub. H.M.S.O. 1955 & 1963.

Cover: Painting of Henry VII by Michael Sittow.
Reproduced by permission of Mansell Collection.

Preface to the Second Edition

The first edition of this Seminar Study was published in 1968, but since that time a great deal of work has been done on the Yorkist and early Tudor period, and many of the interpretations put forward in the first edition are no longer tenable. This second edition, therefore, is not so much a revision of the earlier text as a complete rewriting. It contains a number of new sections, such as those on 'The common law and Chancery' and 'The Church'. It also omits the sections on 'The machinery of government' and 'The weakness of the Crown' which appeared in the earlier version. The main reason for this is the addition to the Seminar Studies Series of David Cook's study of *Lancastrians and Yorkists: The Wars of the Roses*, which deals with the half-century preceding Henry VII's accession.

Roger Lockyer, 1982

Part One: The Background

1 Rural and Urban Society

Fifteenth-century England was not a single economic unit but rather a number of interrelated regional economies. Agriculture was still the main activity, but its practice was not uniform. There was a broad division between the 'highland' zone, which lay to the west of a line from Durham to Weymouth, and the 'lowland' zone of the south and east. The highland zone, as its name implies, included extensive areas of mountains and moorlands, and its thin soils were best suited to pasture farming. The lowland zone, by contrast, had richer soils, suitable for both corn and grass. It was here that the open-field system had reached its maximum development, with large arable fields, broken into strips, surrounded by common pastures and wastes. Another characteristic of this zone was the way in which its inhabitants had settled in tight-knit or 'nuclear' villages, which were integrated into a highly organised manorial system. In the highland zone, on the other hand, the population tended to be scattered in isolated farmsteads or hamlets, and manorial supervision and the communal regulation of agricultural activities were much more difficult to enforce (**62**).

The whole of England, highland and lowland, had been affected by the traumatic decline of population that had occurred largely as a result of the Black Death in the mid-fourteenth century (**71**). As a consequence a great deal of marginal land that had earlier been cultivated was left to return to its natural state. Villages that had no firm economic base were abandoned, and even in those that survived – as well as in the towns, which were so closely linked to the countryside – there were tumbledown buildings that nobody needed, or wished, to occupy.

Attacks of bubonic plague did not come to a sudden halt after the Black Death. On the contrary there were major epidemics about every four years throughout the greater part of the fifteenth century. The last of these came in 1479–80, and thereafter the incidence of plague was less marked and less frequent. It is true that Henry VII's accession coincided with the outbreak of the Sweating Sickness (probably a form of influenza) but although this

1

caused great alarm it was nothing like so deadly as the plague. The late 1470s and the 1480s therefore mark a turning point in English demographic history, for the population slowly began to increase (**84**).

One result of this was growing pressure upon land and natural resources, particularly in the lowland zone, and the profits to be made from efficient farming – now that there were more mouths to feed and wool was commanding record prices – led many landlords to resort to 'enclosure' (see below, p. 58). But the extent of enclosure should not be exaggerated, nor should it be assumed, despite the later assertions of Tudor preachers and pamphleteers, that it was always the consequence of the greed of landlords. Covetous landlords did exist, of course, and caused great suffering, but enclosure was not always or necessarily a disruptive process. In the highland zone much of the land had already been enclosed by the end of the fifteenth century, usually through agreement among the local inhabitants. In the lowland zone the most consistent pressure on resources came not from enclosure but from an increase in the number of livestock let out to graze on the common pastures, and the initiative in this came from enterprising peasants as well as from landlords (**62**).

The pattern of agrarian society, in short, was too complex to allow of easy generalisations, and the course of events was governed to a large extent by unpredictable circumstances. Laziness, illness, or sheer bad luck could hold a man down near subsistence level; but those peasants who were prepared to work hard and had fortune on their side could push their children, if not themselves, into a higher level of society. Clement Paston, for instance, who died in 1419, had only a small farm in Norfolk and married a villein, but he sent his son William to school, even though he had to borrow money to do so. William became a distinguished lawyer, was appointed a judge, and married into a gentry family. The third generation of Pastons were gentry born and carried out the obligations expected of them as knights of the shire and Justices of the Peace.

Although by far the greater part of the English population lived in the countryside, there were some seven hundred towns, ranging in size from London, which had perhaps as many as 50,000 inhabitants, to places like Banbury and Bideford with less than a thousand (**31**). There were only about a hundred medium-sized towns, with populations in the 1,500–5,000 range, and although most of these had flourished during the early fifteenth century a number of them were in decline by the time Henry Tudor came to the throne. York was one of these. It had earlier done well out of the woollen cloth industry, but it suffered, as did other corporate towns, from the exodus of weavers to rural areas – where they were free of restrictive regulations and could supplement their low wages by gathering fuel from the wastes and keeping a few cows or sheep on the common pastures. York also suffered from the decline in its international trade, for the Baltic was closed to English merchants from about 1450, and overseas trade in general was increasingly centred on London. As a result, property values in York collapsed and many buildings were allowed to fall into decay (**97**). Lincoln, Warwick and Northampton are other examples of towns which were in decline.

There was, however, another side to the picture. Southampton, with its fine natural harbour, was becoming one of the principal ports for trade with Italy and the Mediterranean, while further west Exeter was developing into a thriving city and a major regional centre. Norwich was another big town which was flourishing. It doubled its population during the fifteenth century and served as a market for the products of the cloth industry in the surrounding countryside. The making of cloth brought prosperity to smaller places as well. Lavenham, in Suffolk, was one of these, for although it had less than a thousand inhabitants it was among the twelve richest towns in England (**57**). To this day its magnificent church, along with those of Long Melford, Clare and Sudbury, attests the wealth, as well as the devotion, of the Suffolk clothiers.

Towns acted as a magnet for all those people who were driven out of their homes by the twin forces of population pressure and agrarian change. Many found their way to London – and indeed without this steady immigration the population of the capital would have declined, for living conditions there, as in other big towns, were so bad that the death rate always outstripped the rate of live births. The municipal authorities, however, gave a cool welcome to those it described as vagabonds, for it regarded them as a potential threat to order, particularly as there was not enough work to go round. Already in 1475 the municipality had ordered vagabonds and beggars to be expelled from the city, and London's example was followed, before the end of the century, by Coventry and York – declining towns which simply could not cope with the financial burden of poor relief. Local and piecemeal measures such as these, however, were of limited effectiveness, and one of the more intransigent problems facing Henry VII's government was that of trying to control the movement of population from one part of England to another, or at least of limiting its potentially explosive impact (**57**).

2. The Yorkist Inheritance

In 1399 Henry Bolingbroke, Duke of Lancaster, deposed the reigning King of England, Richard II, and seized the throne for himself. Although he thereby established the House of Lancaster as the ruling dynasty he had set an example that other ambitious magnates might one day follow, with fateful consequences for his descendants. Whether or not the Lancastrians maintained their hold on the throne would depend in large part upon their qualities as rulers. Henry V, who succeeded his father in 1413, won prestige for his dynasty by leading an army into France – a kingdom which he claimed as his own – and winning a resounding victory at Agincourt. But Henry died in 1422, leaving as heir his baby son Henry VI. A minority was always a dangerous time for a monarchy, particularly when the ruling house was so recently established, but the magnates who surrounded the young King behaved with remarkable restraint and protected his inheritance for him. It was when Henry came of age that things started to go badly wrong. One reason for this was the fact that the early triumphs in France had given way to defeats, and the financial strain of maintaining the English armies there was causing unrest at home. Another, and more important, reason was Henry's singular lack of the qualities needed to make a successful ruler. He was too easily swayed by those around him, and open-handed to the point of irresponsibility. By giving away royal lands and patronage to those he favoured he blew into flames the smouldering jealousies among the magnates and thereby precipitated violent quarrels between them which he proved unable to resolve (**33, 38, 39**). Henry's incapacity, and occasional lapses into insanity, intensified the fear and ambitions of the leading nobles and led directly to armed conflict between them – the struggles known collectively as the Wars of the Roses. The only possible outcome to these, other than stalemate, was the triumph of one of the magnate factions, and this came about in March 1461, when Edward, Duke of York, destroyed the Lancastrian army at Towton. Just over a year later he was crowned King as Edward IV.

The government of the realm

Edward IV was not yet twenty when he became King, and the energy which his strong physique gave him was reinforced by his determination to be an effective ruler. He had many of the qualities needed for success. He won men to him by his charm and easy manners, while women found his good looks irresistible, but he was no mere playboy. He had a keen business sense, he could be ruthless in the pursuit of his objectives, and he was resolved to restore the royal authority (**93**).

The change of ruler had an immediate effect on the royal Council, which was the major instrument of government. Under Henry VI it had become a virtually autonomous body, dominated by the magnates, and Sir John Fortescue, who was one of Henry's Chief Justices, accurately summarised its weaknesses: 'The King's Council was wont to be chosen of great princes, and of the greatest lords of the land, both spiritual and temporal, and also of other men that were in great authority and offices. Which lords and officers had at hand also many matters of their own to be treated in the Council, as had the King. Wherethrough, when they came together, they were so occupied with their own matters and with the matters of their kin, servants and tenants, that they attended but little, and otherwhile nothing, to the King's matters'(**10** p. 145). Edward rapidly changed this situation. He did not exclude magnates from his Council, as long as he was sure of their loyalty, but he did not allow them to dominate it, and he insisted that they should attend to his business rather than their own. In the period that followed his restoration in 1471 there were some twenty noble Councillors, but many of these were of Edward's own creation, and, as a group, they were smaller than the clerics, who numbered about thirty-five (**94, 95**). Clerics had always played a major part in medieval government because they were literate, they could be rewarded for service to the Crown by promotion in the church, and they left no legitimate heirs to claim a hereditary right to advise the King. Under Edward, as under his predecessors, churchmen occupied major offices of state such as the Lord Chancellorship, but the episcopate was no longer the preserve of the aristocracy. Edward tended to choose as bishops men who came from lesser gentry or merchant families and were therefore dependent on royal favour for their advancement (**59**).

Much the same was true of the third group of Councillors, consisting mainly of officials of the royal household, which numbered eleven in the first part of the reign but increased to twenty-three after 1471 – a sure sign of its increasing importance. The members of this group were drawn from the gentry, the second rank of English society, and had often received a professional training as lawyers or estate administrators. They were already prominent in local government, but under Edward they moved into positions of authority at the centre, and as the Crown's power expanded, so did theirs.

The names of just over a hundred Councillors survive for Edward's reign but they never all met together. In practice the Council consisted of anything from nine to twelve members, and the maximum recorded attendance was twenty. The King summoned whom he liked when he liked, and although the Council would, if Edward so wished, discuss major issues and make recommendations, he accepted or rejected these as he saw fit (**59, 94, 95**).

While Edward's accession meant a sharp decline in the influence of the magnates on royal government, the new King was by no means anti-aristocratic. As a magnate himself Edward felt at ease among the company of his fellow nobles, and during the course of his reign he created over thirty peerages. A number of these new peers held important offices at court – William Hastings, for instance, who was made a baron in 1461, was Lord Chamberlain of the household for the whole of Edward's reign – but their major role, like that of the old nobles, was to maintain order in the localities, and Edward deliberately built up aristocratic influence where he believed it could serve his purpose. He presented Hastings with large grants of confiscated property in the midlands; he gave William Herbert lands and offices to establish his predominance in Wales; and in the second part of his reign he made his brother, Richard, Duke of Gloucester, the greatest magnate in the north (**52**).

Edward did not rely solely on the nobles to act as links between the court and the localities. He also used members of his household – in particular the Knights and Esquires of the Body, who numbered about fifty by the end of his reign. These came mainly from established gentry families, and when they were not doing their turn of duty at court they would retire to their country estates. Their presence in the countryside was in itself a stabilising influence, and they helped restore the machinery of local government and made it function more effectively (**59**). Yet the maintenance of good order continued to be a problem throughout Edward's

7

reign, for the effects of the civil wars did not disappear overnight and Edward made little attempt to curb retaining, which was a major source of disorder since it allowed his greater subjects to employ what were in effect private armies. However, when disorder became a major threat to the security of his throne Edward would act swiftly and decisively. During the first part of his reign in particular he made extensive use of the Constable's Court, or Court of Chivalry, which, under the ruthless leadership of John Tiptoft, Earl of Worcester and Constable of England, dealt in a summary fashion with those it deemed guilty of insurrection. Edward also issued frequent commissions of oyer and terminer, which empowered those appointed to them to put down riots and other breaches of the peace. These commissions would usually include Councillors, household officials, nobles and judges whose combined authority was calculated to overawe all but the most arrogant offenders (**59**). Edward was not content merely to act by deputies, however. He was always on the move, travelling in state from one disturbed region to another and using the majesty of his kingly office as well as his own abundant energy to impose order. In some instances – particularly when his own adherents were themselves the cause of unrest – Edward preferred to turn a blind eye to what was going on, but in general he took a firm stand and demonstrated beyond any shadow of doubt his determination to be obeyed.

3 Financial Administration

The weakness of royal government in the mid-fifteenth century had sprung, in large part, from shortage of money. The first Lancastrian had enjoyed a revenue of some £90,000 annually, but by the closing years of Henry VI this had diminished to £24,000 (**59**). Edward realised that in order to make the Crown strong once again he would have to restore it to solvency, but this turned out to be a slow process. He could have called on Parliament for assistance, but Parliament had become a focus for opposition to the monarch during the Lancastrian period and he may well have thought that a break with the past implied a reduction in its role. He summoned only six Parliaments during a reign of twenty-three years, and he assured members in 1467 that 'I purpose to live upon mine own, and not to charge my subjects but in great and urgent causes concerning the weal of themselves and also the defence of them and of this my realm, rather than my own pleasure'. Edward was as good as his word, for although he received nearly £190,000 in Parliamentary taxation during the course of his reign he used this to meet the 'extraordinary' costs of suppressing rebellions at home and waging war abroad.

As far as the 'ordinary' revenue was concerned, Edward was dependent on his own resources. When he seized the Crown he acquired the royal estates, including those of the Duchy of Lancaster, and he also held extensive properties in his own right as Duke of York. Furthermore he persuaded Parliament to pass four Acts of resumption which recovered for the Crown a good deal of the land which Henry VI had alienated. The mere possession of property, however, was no guarantee of wealth: the Crown lands needed to be administered in such a way that they would yield a substantial and increasing profit. The medieval monarchy had developed, in the Exchequer, a sophisticated and elaborate mechanism for collecting and auditing the King's revenues, but its procedure was slow and during the civil wars it had fallen badly behind. Edward wanted to exercise the same close, personal control over his revenues that he did over policy-making, and for this reason he increasingly by-passed the Exchequer and made the royal Chamber – which had hitherto dealt only with the finances of the court and household – into a national treasury.

From early in his reign Edward began the practice of removing lands from Exchequer control and placing them instead under specially appointed receivers and surveyors who accounted to the Chamber. Sir Thomas Vaughan, the Treasurer of the Chamber, thereby became a key figure in the administration of the royal finances, but Edward himself took an active part, inspecting the Chamber accounts and giving Vaughan instructions by word of mouth. 'By 1483,' in the words of Edward's biographer, 'there had emerged a system of highly personal financial control, centred on the Chamber, which anticipated in all essentials the structure once thought to have been created by the early Tudors' (**59** p. 375).

Edward had other sources of ordinary revenue apart from the Crown lands. In 1465 Parliament voted him the Customs duties for life and as foreign trade expanded with the return of more settled conditions the Customs became increasingly valuable. By the end of the reign they were bringing in some £34,000 a year, which was considerably more than the net yield from the royal estates. Edward also enforced his feudal rights, especially wardship, but he had to tread carefully here since he risked provoking a hostile reaction on the part of the landowners. Another source of income, after 1475, was the pension of £10,000 a year which the King of France agreed to pay Edward in return for an end of hostilities (see below, p. 71), and Edward also made substantial profits through engaging in trading ventures on his own account. The result of all this activity was that by 1475 Edward was solvent – the first English sovereign to be so for more than a century – and by the time he died he had pushed the royal revenue up to around £70,000 a year – still not as high as that of Henry IV but nearly three times what it had been at the time of Edward's accession (**59**).

Part Two: Analysis

4   The New King

The brief rule of the Yorkists came to an end in August 1485, when Henry Tudor defeated and killed Edward's successor, Richard III, at the battle of Bosworth. Henry was the posthumous son of Edmund Tudor, who had been created Earl of Richmond by his half-brother Henry VI. Edmund's mother was Catherine of France, who had first been married to Henry V and, after his death, took as her second husband one of her household officers, Owen Tudor, who belonged to an old Welsh family. Henry's effective claim to the throne came, however, through his mother, Margaret Beaufort, who was descended from Edward III through the marriage of his third son, John of Gaunt, Duke of Lancaster, to Catherine Swynford (see family tree, p. 103). But Catherine's children had been born before she became the legitimate wife of John of Gaunt, and although an Act of Parliament in Richard II's reign removed the stain of illegitimacy from the Beauforts, Henry IV had a clause inserted excluding them from any claim to the throne.

Henry was born in January 1457 at Pembroke Castle and was brought up by his uncle Jasper Tudor, Earl of Pembroke. However, after the defeat and subsequent murder of Henry VI in 1471 it seemed safer for Henry, who was now head of the house of Lancaster, to move out of the Yorkists' range. He and Jasper therefore fled to Brittany. Henry spent fourteen years in exile, waiting for a suitable opportunity to return and claim his inheritance. In autumn 1483 the moment seemed to have arrived, for Henry planned a landing in England to coincide with the Duke of Buckingham's rebellion against Richard III. But the rebellion broke out prematurely, Buckingham was captured and executed, and although Henry set sail his ships were dispersed in a storm, and when he arrived off the English coast he decided not to land.

The triumphant Richard now put pressure on the Duke of Brittany to hand over the troublesome exile, and Henry had to take refuge in France. There he planned a further invasion attempt, this time in his homeland of Wales where he could hope for a favourable reception. In August 1485 he landed in Milford Haven, not far from his birthplace, and marched rapidly inland. He had a small band of mercenaries with him, which was increased by a steady trickle of volunteers as he moved through Wales. But there was no general rising in his favour, and he would have stood little chance of defeating Richard's army as long as it remained faithful to the King. Richard's cause, however, aroused no more enthusiasm than Henry's. Only nine nobles, less than a quarter of the English baronage, joined Richard at Bosworth, and not all of these were firmly committed to him (**51**). Henry hoped – not without good reason – that when the moment of decision came some of them would hold back or even switch their allegiance. A key figure in his calculations was Thomas, Lord Stanley, who had become the third husband of Lady Margaret Beaufort and was therefore Henry's stepfather. Stanley deliberately avoided committing his forces to the battle. So at first did his brother, Sir William Stanley. But at the crucial moment, when Henry was losing ground, Sir William sent his three thousand men to attack Richard in the rear. Richard knew the game was up. With a cry of 'Treachery!' he plunged into the heart of the battle and was struck down. The circlet of gold which adorned his brow fell off and was picked up by Lord Stanley, who placed it on Henry's head. Richard's naked body was slung over a horse and carried ignominiously away to Leicester, where it was buried (**9**).

Henry VII, who was now, at the age of twenty-eight, King of England, was a virtual stranger to his kingdom, having spent the first part of his life in Wales and the rest in exile. He was slim, taller than average, and his face, with its straight, Roman nose, its pronounced cheekbones, and its large hooded eyes, was one of considerable nobility [**doc. 1**] We are accustomed to think of Henry as a silent, grave man, whose countenance, as Bacon said 'was reverend, and a little like a churchman', but this is only part of the picture. It is true that he cultivated discretion to such a point that men could never be certain what he was thinking, but he also had something of his granddaughter Elizabeth's liveliness of wit, and he was very fond of music, buying organs and lutes for his family. 'For his pleasures,' says Bacon, 'there is no news of them', but Henry was far from ascetic, nor was he miserly where the dignity of the crown was concerned. When the old royal palace of Sheen was destroyed by fire he replaced it with a new one which he named in honour of his Yorkshire earldom of Richmond – though his subjects called it Rich Mount because of the large sums of money spent on its construction and furnishings. Richmond covered ten acres and was surmounted by a cluster of onion-shaped domes, each with its gilded weather-vane decorated with the royal arms (**35**). Nothing but the gatehouse now remains, and nothing at all of Baynard's Castle, another medieval palace which Henry rebuilt (**107**). He also carried out extensive works at the palace of Placentia, overlooking the Thames at Greenwich, but these were all swept away when Wren and Hawksmoor created the present buildings. Yet some idea of the richness and quality of Henry's creations is to be gained from two of his achievements which have survived: the chapel of King's College, Cambridge, which he brought to completion, and the jewel-like lady chapel which he added to Westminster Abbey, and which bears his name.

Like many English monarchs before and after him, Henry was passionately addicted to hunting and to country life in general, and he took particular delight in exotic animals, establishing a menagerie at the Tower, with lions, leopards, wild cats and rare birds. He enjoyed playing cards and dicing, and had an endearing weakness for clowns and buffoons. Visitors to his court encountered there, among other and more distinguished personages, 'the foolyshe duc of Lancastre', Dego the Spanish jester, and Scot and Dick the master fools (**53**). It would be a mistake, however, to assume that buffoonery was the keynote of Henry's court. On the contrary, he insisted on a high degree of formality, and consciously cultivated 'magnificence', taking as his model the Dukes of Burgundy, whose court was generally regarded as the finest in all Christendom. 'Magnificence' implied not simply rich costumes and elaborate ceremonial but also the encouragement of artists and men of letters so that the court would become the principal focus of cultural activity. Edward IV, for instance, had purchased books and tapestries in an unsystematic manner, but Henry became an avid and discerning collector of both. He was not content to leave his books in the custody of the Wardrobe, as his predecessor had done, but established the royal library as a separate department of the household, and appointed a Keeper to run it (**49**).

Henry's library contained few English or Latin books; its great strength lay in its collections of histories, romances and verse epics written mainly in French, and in its fine illuminated manuscripts. Indeed it was the existence of the royal library that led to the setting up of a school of Flemish illustrators at the English court. Among the poets patronised by Henry were John Skelton, whom he appointed tutor to Prince Henry, and Bernard André, the blind poet from Toulouse, whom he made the official court chronicler.

In the words of one historian, 'no previous English King had been so acutely aware of the political advantages of surrounding himself with literary servants' whose task was 'to present Tudor policy in as forceful and impressive a manner as possible' (**49** p. 132).

Further evidence of Burgundian influence was to be seen in the collection of tapestries which Henry assembled and which did much to enhance the visual splendour of his court. He also used Flemish craftsmen to enrich his palaces with stained glass, and turned the office of King's Glazier into an autonomous department of the royal household: an enduring monument to his discriminating patronage is to be seen in the superb Flemish glass in the windows of King's College chapel. Henry extended his patronage to troupes of actors, drawn from the household, and took great delight in the performance of pageants, in which speech, music, dance and spectacle were interwoven in a way that looked forward to the Stuart masques. Related to the pageants were the tournaments, stylised encounters with romantic and allegorical overtones, which Henry also actively encouraged. In 1506 he was able to display the newly acquired skills of the Tudor court in this particular art form to no less a person than the Duke of Burgundy himself (**49**).

Henry's admiration for Burgundy, which led him to patronise Flemish writers and artists, did not mean that he was impervious to the influence of the Italian renaissance. For example he appointed the poet Peter Carmelianus, who had been born in Brescia, to the newly created post of Latin secretary, and he commissioned Polydore Vergil, a native of Urbino, to write a history of England (**43**). These men were humanists, in the sense that their learning was firmly rooted in the classics, particularly Latin, but because they came at this early stage, when Renaissance influences were only slowly beginning to make their effect felt on England, they were later overshadowed by greater figures. Much the same is true of Henry's cultural achievement as a whole, for his commitment to Burgundy, so natural at the time, seemed old-fashioned and even obscurantist to the next generation of humanists. Yet he contributed a great deal that was of enduring value to English culture, and by spending substantial sums of money he 'transformed the royal household into a major influence upon the development of the fine arts in England. By the same means, he set a standard of courtly patronage and established a distinctive royal style for his descendants' (**49** p. 164).

5 Finance

Exchequer and Chamber

That Henry was fond of money is widely known, but this was more than a miser's senseless addiction. He told Henry Wyatt – one of his Councillors and father of the poet, Sir Thomas Wyatt – that 'the Kings my predecessors, weakening their treasure, have made themselves servants to their subjects', and it was apparent to any intelligent observer that the effectiveness of royal government depended to a large extent upon its wealth.

Henry was no innovator when it came to financial matters. For one thing he knew that any proposal to raise money from new sources would arouse suspicion and probably provoke the disorder he was so anxious to avoid. And, for another, the Yorkists had shown that the existing revenues could be expanded sufficiently to give him the financial strength he needed. Consciously or unconsciously he followed the example of Edward IV, of whom one chronicler says 'he turned all his thoughts to the question of how he might in future collect, out of his own substance and by the exercise of his own energy, an amount of treasure worthy of his royal station'.

Henry began, like Edward IV, with a general Act of Resumption, which was passed in 1486 and nominally restored to the Crown all the lands which it had held in October 1455. There were, however, many exemptions to this statute, and although a second Act of Resumption was passed in the following year, Henry really laid claim to little more than Richard III had held. The main object of these Acts was not to give Henry possession of his subjects' property but to make sure that in the many cases where ownership was uncertain and disputed the Crown would be well placed to assert its own claims. Henry's first parliament assured him the revenues of the Duchies of Lancaster and Cornwall and the Earldoms of Richmond and Chester, and constant additions to the royal lands were made throughout the reign by the use of Acts of attainder (see p. 50) against the King's enemies. Just under 140 individuals suffered in this way during Henry's reign, and although a third of the attainders were reversed the net effect was a considerable transfer of property to the Crown (**29, 92**). Among Henry's greatest gains was the estate of Sir William Stanley which brought in £9,000 in cash and £1,000 a year, and the steady addition of attainted estates, as well as the exploitation of established rights, put a considerable strain upon the existing financial machinery.

The system of Chamber finance which the Yorkists had developed could only work satisfactorily if the King actively supervised it. Henry VII, however, had no experience in financial administration, and was in any case fully occupied with securing his hold upon his newly-won throne. The collection and auditing of the Crown's revenues might have broken down altogether had not the Exchequer resumed its earlier and traditional role as guardian of the royal finances. But it had not been designed to deal with the complexities of fifteenth-century estate administration and had neither the personnel nor the techniques to cope with the tasks confronting it. As a consequence the Crown's income from land declined from about £25,000 *per annum* at the end of Richard III's reign to less than £12,000 in the first year of Henry's (**52**). This situation lasted until the early 1490s, by which time Henry felt himself secure enough to turn his attention to financial matters. Impelled by the same determination to establish personal control over the Crown finances that had motivated Edward IV, Henry was driven to reconstruct the Yorkist system. More and more revenues were withdrawn from Exchequer control, and by the end of Henry's reign the Chamber was once again the major national treasury, receiving some 90 per cent of all the Crown's income.

The transformation of the Chamber from a household department into a national treasury led to the emergence of a Secret or Privy Chamber, whose chief officer – indeed for some time its only one – was the Groom of the Stool. He acted in effect as keeper of the King's privy purse, paying out 'rewards' on Henry's behalf and making whatever purchases the King needed for his private use. In other words, as the Chamber moved 'out of court' the functions which it had previously performed in connexion with the less formal, or private, aspects of the King's life were taken over by the Privy Chamber, and the Groom of the Stool supervised those elements of household finance which the Treasurer of the Chamber no longer had time for (**61**).

One of the disadvantages of using the Chamber as a national treasury was that it did not possess the elaborate auditing machinery which the Exchequer had developed over the course of its long history. Edward IV had appointed *ad hoc* auditors to examine those accounts which were no longer to be submitted to Exchequer scrutiny, and for some time Henry continued this practice, while acting himself as his own chief auditor. The head of the Chamber was its Treasurer, a post held from 1492 onwards by John Heron. He presented his accounts regularly to the King, who inspected them closely and signified his approval by initialling them. Without this close personal supervision the system of Chamber finance could never have worked as well as it did, but although Henry maintained his tight control he came increasingly to rely upon the advice and assistance of Sir Reginald Bray, who was one of his few close friends. Bray had learnt the business of estate management as surveyor and receiver-general to Sir Henry Stafford, and he entered royal service as a consequence of Stafford's marriage to the widowed Lady Margaret Beaufort, the mother of Henry VII. After Henry became King he appointed Bray Chancellor of the Duchy of Lancaster, thereby making him responsible for administering one of the greatest landed estates in the kingdom. Duchy procedures had become somewhat lethargic as a result of the political upheaval that accompanied Richard III's overthrow, but Bray quickly breathed new life into them by appointing special commissioners to enquire into cases of neglect or delay. This confirmed Henry's high opinion of him and he became the King's chief adviser on financial matters (**21**).

It was Bray, therefore, who assumed the responsibility for developing new auditing machinery for the Chamber. He worked in co-operation with Heron and a number of other household officials, and he instituted the practice of holding regular meetings at which the Chamber accounts were submitted to intensive scrutiny. After Bray's death in 1503 his place was taken by Sir Robert Southwell, who was assisted by the Bishop of Carlisle and a dozen or so other officials, most of them members either of the royal Council or of the Prince of Wales's household. As early as the mid-1490s this committee of auditors was being referred to as the 'General Surveyors', but in fact a formally constituted Court of General Surveyors did not come into existence until Henry VIII's reign. Nevertheless, Southwell and his associates functioned as an informal court of audit, developing routines for examining local receivers and going through their accounts before submitting them to the King (**85**).

Feudal and prerogative revenue

Moneys paid into the Chamber came from two main sources. First of all there were the revenues from estates such as the Duchies of Lancaster and Cornwall, which, from about 1487 onwards, were withdrawn from Exchequer control. These revenues were swelled by those from lands which passed to the Crown during Henry's reign by attainder or escheat. Secondly there were the profits from the exploitation of the Crown's prerogative. There were two main aspects to this prerogative. In the first place the King, as the greatest of all feudal lords, could claim the rights which belonged, by ancient custom to any lord. Should he be unfortunate enough to be captured and held to ransom, he could demand an aid to raise the necessary sum. He could also call for aids on the occasion of the marriage of his eldest daughter and the knighting of his eldest son. Feudal aids could not be levied without the consent of the tenants-in-chief (which meant, in practice, of Parliament), but no consent was needed for the feudal incidents, of which the most important was wardship. If a tenant-in-chief died leaving an under-age heir, the boy became a ward of the King and his estates passed under royal guardianship – to compensate the King for the loss of military service implicit in the succession of a minor. In practice the King usually sold the wardship to the highest bidder, and there was no shortage of takers since the man who acquired guardianship of a ward usually assumed control of the boy's estates as well. The guardian was forbidden by law to despoil the estates for which he was responsible, but 'despoiling' was an uncertain term, and the high price paid for wardships suggests that those who bought them calculated on making a substantial profit. Wardship did not necessarily involve the intervention of a third party, however. A mother or other relative could apply for the guardianship of the minor, and the request might well be granted – but only, of course, upon payment.

Although wardship was the most lucrative of the feudal incidents to which the King was entitled, it was not the only one. When a ward came of age he had to pay a due called 'Livery' before he could take control of his inheritance. If the heir was a woman, the King had the right to control her marriage and this was also a source of profit. The King would either sell the right to marry the heiress, or, if she was rich enough, would sell her the privilege of deciding her own fate. If there was no heir, the King would claim the right of escheat, and take the lands back into his own hands.

He could exercise this right also if a tenant-in-chief was found to be a lunatic or an idiot. The theory behind all these incidents dated from the earlier medieval period, when the military organisation of the country really did depend upon the knight-service of tenants-in-chief. By the time Henry came to the throne indentured retainers and commissions of array had replaced feudal obligations as the most effective way of raising armies, but feudalism, although deprived of its *raison d'être*, remained in existence as a financial system [**doc. 2**].

From early on in his reign Henry appointed commissioners to investigate the extent of his feudal rights. Laboriously but inexorably they pursued their enquiries, ferreting out under-age heirs whose existence had been concealed in an attempt to evade wardship. The last fifty 'Inquisitions Post-Mortem' for Henry's reign record the discovery of twenty-eight under-age heirs. The average life span was short in early Tudor England: hence the frequency of inheritance by minors, and the significance of wardship. Where the tenure by which estates were held was disputed or uncertain, the commissioners would invariably rule in favour of the Crown, but the landowners had a right of appeal to the common law courts. In 1505, for instance, a royal commission in Northumberland declared that twenty tenancies of the Earl of Northumberland belonged in fact to the Crown; but King's Bench, on an appeal by the tenants, reversed most of these verdicts (**4, 21, 99**).

As a result of Henry's remorseless pressure his income from wardship rose substantially. In 1487 he obtained less than £300 from this source, but by 1494 receipts were running at over £1,500 and by 1507 they had soared to more than £6,000 a year. At first Henry appointed household officials *ad hoc* to deal with wardship, but as the revenue increased the need for specialisation became apparent. This was especially the case after the death of Bray in 1503, and it was no coincidence that the same year saw the creation of the office of Master of Wards, with the responsibility for 'overseeing, managing and selling the wardships of all lands which may be in the King's hands'. Sir John Hussey, the first Master, quickly built up an organisation and by 1509 there were probably local masters, receivers-general and auditors in every county, all responsible to Hussey, who was of course responsible to the King (**58**).

In addition to his feudal prerogative the King had privileges which belonged to him as King. As the guardian of his subjects, for instance, he had the right – indeed the duty – to make them live in peace and good order, to punish those who resisted, to take bonds of good behaviour, and to supplement the course of the common law where it was deficient. All aspects of the prerogative, feudal and non-feudal alike, had this in common, that they were potential sources of profit, and the responsibility for enforcing prerogative rights was therefore assumed by Bray and his associates in the informal court of audit (**85**). After Bray's death, however, and with the creation of a separate department of wards, there was no one specifically responsible for enforcing prerogative rights other than wardship. Henry filled this gap, in August 1508, by creating a new office of Surveyor of the King's Prerogative and appointing Sir Edward Belknap to it (**99**). Belknap had a mixed bag of duties. One of his principal tasks was to seek out widows of tenants-in-chief who had re-married without first obtaining leave from the King, and to exact a financial penalty from them. He was also required to improve the effectiveness of common law procedures by seizing the lands of all those who had been convicted of felonies or murder, or had been outlawed for failing to comply with the orders of the courts. In addition the King instructed Belknap to collect debts that were owing to the Crown, as well as fines which the King himself often assessed for breaches of the law. Much of this activity overlapped with that of the Council Learned (see p. 25), and Belknap in fact worked hand in hand with Empson and Dudley. It was this association with men who came to be identified with the more extortionate aspects of Henry's rule that led to the winding-up of the office of Surveyor of the King's Prerogative early in Henry VIII's reign.

Henry's financial achievement

Because of the complexities of Tudor accounting systems it is not possible to give any exact figures for Henry's finances, but it seems likely that during the course of his reign the income from royal lands and wardship went up 45 per cent from £29,000 to £42,000 while the Customs revenue increased by just over 20 per cent, from £33,000 to £40,000 (**68**). By the end of the reign the Chamber was handling well over £90,000 a year while another £12,500 went to the Exchequer. If a further £10,000 is added for miscellaneous sources of revenue, Henry's total annual income works out at something over £113,000 (**105**). The fact that this was nearly three times as large as Henry VI's in the mid-1430s in an indication of the success of the Yorkists and the first Tudor in restoring the royal finances. Yet the royal income had been substantially higher in the pre-Lancastrian period. Richard II probably received £120,000 *per annum*, while his grandfather, Edward III, had for a brief period enjoyed a revenue of £160,000. In other words the Yorkist and early Tudor achievement consisted in restoring the Crown's finances to the relatively healthy state they had been in prior to 1399 (**52, 66**).

The bare statistics of monies received do not, of course, give a complete picture of the financial situation. Certain revenues – varying in amount from the thousands of pounds paid annually to the Treasurer of Calais by the Company of the Staple to the small sums which sheriffs and other royal officials were allowed to deduct from their receipts for their salaries and expenses – never passed through the central receiving agencies. The King also had a 'concealed income', for when he rewarded one of his servants by granting him a lucrative office or selling him a wardship at a nominal sum he was saving himself money, and this was, in effect, a form of income. But even when generous allowance has been made for all these indirect sources of profit to the Crown it is unlikely that Henry VII's revenue came anywhere near the £1,100,000 enjoyed by the Emperor, or even the £800,000 which the King of France could expect every year.

By about 1490 Henry was solvent, and thereafter he enjoyed, in Bacon's phrase, 'the felicity of full coffers'. It was rumoured that he left a substantial fortune for his heir to squander but in fact the Chamber contained only £9,000 in cash at the time of his death. There may have been other, unrecorded, sums in the hands of the Groom of the Stool (**61**), and the plate and jewels in which Henry had invested were worth many thousands of pounds, but even when these are taken into account they do not add up to a 'fortune'. Recognition of Henry VII's undoubted and major achievement in restoring the royal finances must not, therefore, obscure the fundamental truth that by European standards the English monarchy was under-endowed, circumscribed in its freedom of action, and dependent upon a considerable degree of co-operation – however grudgingly given – from those who were subject to it.

6 Administration

The Council

Henry VII's Council, in its composition and range of activities, was virtually the same as that of his immediate predecessors, and indeed twenty-nine of his Councillors had held the same office under one or both of the Yorkist Kings (**29**). The largest group within the Council consisted of clerics, and among Henry's most trusted advisers was John Morton, whom he appointed Archbishop of Canterbury in 1486 and Lord Chancellor the following year. Morton had been involved in Buckingham's rebellion against Richard III and had subsequently fled to join Henry in exile. He was a man of outstanding ability, played a major part in government, and continued to enjoy Henry's confidence down to the time of his death in 1500. Another former exile who became a prominent figure on the Council was Richard Fox, whom Henry chose as his secretary. In 1487 Fox was given the bishopric of Exeter as well as the office of Lord Keeper of the Privy Seal, and Henry made frequent use of him on diplomatic missions.

The nobles were also represented on the Council, and there was no sign under Henry VII any more than there had been under Edward IV of a deliberate attempt to oust them from government. Ability and loyalty were the only prerequisites as far as Henry was concerned, and his Council therefore included John de Vere, thirteenth Earl of Oxford, who had stood by his side at Bosworth and was rewarded with the offices of Lord Great Chamberlain and Lord Admiral. Henry did not confine membership of the Council to those nobles who had fought for him. Thomas Howard, Earl of Surrey, had been among Richard's adherents at Bosworth and had suffered for his loyalty to the Yorkist cause by being imprisoned in the Tower. After three years' captivity, however, he was released and appointed to the Council, and Henry gave a further demonstration of trust in him by sending Surrey to the north to put down a rising that had been sparked off by the murder of another of Henry's noble servants, the Earl of Northumberland. In 1501, following the death of Lord Dinham, Henry appointed Surrey to the major office of Lord Treasurer.

The Lord Chancellor, the Lord Privy Seal and the Lord Treasurer formed the core of Henry's Council, along with five other members who held minor offices or none at all. These included Giles Daubeny, another former exile whom Henry created a baron in 1486. This was virtually the only new creation of Henry's reign, for the King was extremely niggardly when it came to giving his followers peerages; the most they could hope for was appointment to the Order of the Garter – a great honour, of course, but not hereditary – and of nearly forty new Knights of the Garter in Henry's reign more than half were men who had served him in government (**29**).

To the extent that Henry was reluctant to grant hereditary titles and thereby build up a new aristocracy, the traditional picture of him as a ruler who distrusted the nobility is valid. His chief secular advisers were drawn not from the aristocracy but from lesser landowners and professional men, especially lawyers. These were 'middle class' in the sense that they were lower in degree than the nobles and higher than the masses, but the term is too misleading to be of value. In their aspirations and assumptions, and often indeed in their family connexions, they were very close to the landed aristocracy and formed part of the upper section of English society. They were 'new' only to the extent that their ancestors had not been numbered among the principal servants of the Crown in previous centuries; but in local government they had generations of experience and prestige behind them. Of the five non-clerical 'core' members of the Council, for instance, Daubeny was the descendant of a peer, Sir Richard Guildford was the son of a Kentish knight, Sir Thomas Lovell of a Norfolk landowner, and Sir John Risely of a Buckinghamshire gentleman, while Sir Reginald Bray came from an old Norman family.

Among Councillors who emerged later in the reign, Edmund Dudley was the grandson of a Lancastrian peer; Sir Edward Belknap's family traced its descent from one of William the Conqueror's companions in arms; while Sir Edward Poynings's father was a Kentish squire and his mother a Paston. Sir Richard Empson seems to have been the only 'new man' on Henry's Council who came from a 'bourgeois' background, but even in his case the term is misleading, since although his father was a leading citizen of

Towcester he also owned property in the surrounding countryside (**106**). In effect, then, Henry's Councillors came from gentry families and made their way in the world through estate management, or the law (or both). So much of Henry's income derived from his lands that he needed men who were skilled in managing property and conversant with the intricacies of land law. These qualifications, rather than social position, were the characteristics of his lay Councillors.

The names of just under 230 Councillors have been recorded for Henry's reign, but they were scattered throughout the country and were irregular in their attendance: indeed, more than forty of them apparently never attended a Council meeting. Of the total number, 27 per cent were clerics, 22 per cent officials, 20 per cent courtiers, 19 per cent peers and 12 per cent lawyers – though these categories are not mutually exclusive and the figures give only a general indication of the make-up of the Council (**29**). The two Chief Justices – of King's Bench and Common Pleas – were frequent attenders, and the King himself was also often present. The Council began work early in the new reign and by the summer of 1486 it was holding regular formal meetings during the law terms in the room known as the Star Chamber. It was particularly concerned with problems of internal security, the defence of the realm and foreign affairs, and there was real debate at its sessions, even though the ultimate decision on whether and how to implement the Council's recommendations rested with the King (**42**).

The number of Councillors present at any meeting varied from four to forty, with seven as the commonest. The key figures were, of course, the holders of major offices, and the prestige of the Council was increased by the fact that Henry kept his ministers in power for long periods – a demonstration of confidence which helped them to build up their own authority. From 1487 until the end of the reign there were only two Lord Chancellors, who between them held office for over twenty years. Lord Dinham was Treasurer until his death in 1501, and thereafter Surrey; while Richard Fox occupied the post of Lord Keeper of the Privy Seal from 1487 onwards. These men gave stability to the new regime, for as their authority increased it underpinned that of the Crown (**55**).

Although the Council was the most important single administrative institution it did not concern itself with every aspect of government. Fiscal policy, for instance, and the enforcement of prerogative rights were handled informally by a group consisting of Bray, Lovell, Morton and Fox, in company with the King. After the deaths of Morton and Bray these tasks were taken over by the Council Learned and the informal court of audit which supervised the Chamber accounts (**42**).

The Council also left law enforcement largely in the hands of more specialised tribunals, such as the one established by statute in 1487 (see below p. 29). This statute was later given the erroneous title '*Pro Camera Stellata*' and was held to be the origin of the Court of Star Chamber, but in fact the 1487 tribunal was quite distinct from the Council in Star Chamber, though there was some overlap of personnel. It was simply one of a number of bodies which emerged in Henry's reign to deal with specific aspects of administration.

The organisation of the Council was in practice very fluid. Small groups of Councillors might be working on different problems in different places, but this did not mean that they ceased to be members of the parent body. One of the major splits was between those Councillors who stayed behind at Westminster when the King went on progress, and those who accompanied him; but when the King returned, the Councillors attendant made their way once more to the Star Chamber, and the two groups never developed into separate institutions (**29, 42**). Only in relatively few cases did specialisation lead to the emergence of what were, in effect, autonomous bodies. The clearest instance of this was the Council Learned.

The Council Learned

The Council Learned was a small body, with a maximum of twelve members, though they never all met together. The great majority of members had received a legal training and were therefore 'learned in law' – hence the name given to this council. It had close connexions with the Duchy of Lancaster, whose Chancellor acted as a kind of president, and its meetings usually took place in the Duchy Chamber. The Council Learned was in existence from at least 1495 (**106**), and Bray, as Chancellor of the Duchy, played a prominent part in its proceedings. But its reputation – or rather its notoriety – increased after Sir Richard Empson became Chancellor of the Duchy in 1504. Empson was a lawyer, and his close associate was Edmund Dudley, a former under-sheriff of London who became Speaker in 1504. It should, however, be borne in mind that Empson and Dudley were friends and colleagues of Bray, and had presumably learnt many of their methods from him (**29, 72, 101**).

Most of the cases with which the Council Learned was involved arose out of its own initiative, for it dealt with a wide range of prosecutions on behalf of the Crown, and also acted as a debt-collecting agency for it. As far as this latter function was concerned it operated in effect as the enforcement arm of the Chamber, which did not have either the legal expertise or the coercive powers to handle debt collection itself, and was fully stretched in coping with its vastly enlarged responsibilities as a national treasury. There may seem, on the face of it, little connexion between debt-collecting and the handling of Crown prosecutions, but the King's profit was common to both and explains why they went together (**29**). Where prosecutions were concerned, the Council Learned dealt with a wide variety of offences – for instance, the export of wool without paying Customs dues, the transference of land to a corporation without licence of mortmain, the failure to take up knighthood, the misconduct of sheriffs, and the infringement of the King's rights of wardship and livery (**101**).

The complaints made against the Council Learned were that it operated without a jury and that too much discretion was left to its members where the fixing of penalties was involved. There was nothing exceptional about operating without a jury, of course: this was true of conciliar activity as a whole, and had come about because of the frequency with which juries were suborned by interested parties. As for the lack of certainty about penalties, this depended upon the nature of the offence. Where these concerned penal statutes (see below, p. 52) the fine might be fixed by law; but where offences against the royal prerogative were involved the penalty was a matter for the King's discretion. This also applied to that part of the Council Learned's business which affected those who wanted a favour from the King, such as hiring one of his ships, or asking him not to enforce his rights in the event of wardship or lunacy [**doc. 3**].

The Council Learned was also involved in the drawing up of bonds and recognisances, binding the persons concerned to good behaviour under threat of a financial penalty. The use of such instruments was not uncommon at a time when legal procedures were ineffective. Edward IV had employed them to hold the magnates in check, but Henry went one stage further and imposed them on the greater part of the English aristocracy (**96**). Out of sixty-two peerage families in existence during his reign forty-six or seven were, for a greater or lesser period 'at the King's mercy', either through Acts of attainder (which Henry was much less willing to reverse than Edward had been) or, more commonly, through bonds and recognisances [**doc. 4**]. In the words of one historian 'never before . . . had any monarch developed the disciplinary use of such financial instruments to so systematic and involved a degree' (**51** p. 292).

Henry, in effect, put the peerage on probation, and the penalties he imposed for anti-social behaviour could be substantial: in 1504, to take one example, the Earl of Northumberland and the Archbishop of York were both commanded to give bonds of £2,000 to keep the peace towards each other. Some peers were required to enter into more than one recognisance. The unfortunate Earl of Shrewsbury gave bonds totalling about £500 on his own behalf, and later on bound himself in respect of the good behaviour of some of his friends, with the result that by the end of the reign he was standing as surety for five different groups of people and was 'endangered' for more than £5,000. This method of preserving peace was no doubt effective, but to the nobles who were its victims it seemed like blackmail. There was little they could do about it while Henry lived, but they focused their resentment on Empson and Dudley, who were his instruments, and the Council Learned through which they worked.

Empson and Dudley were undoubtedly ruthless in their enforcement of royal rights (**106**); they were accused, among other things, of falsely asserting that certain lands were held by feudal tenure, and therefore subject to wardship and other incidents which were profitable to the King but vexatious to his subjects [**doc. 5**]. They were also occasionally guilty of corrupt practices. Thomas Sunnyff, for instance, was accused by one of Dudley's men of murdering his (stillborn) child, and Dudley demanded payment of £500, saying 'Agree with the King, or else you must go to the Tower.' When Sunnyff refused he was imprisoned, and although he appealed to the common law the judges rejected his plea for bail on the grounds that they could not disregard the King's commands. Sunnyff eventually paid up, for fear that he would otherwise rot in prison until he died. Dudley later expressed remorse for his action, but insisted that he had made not a penny out of it: all the money went to the King (**76, 79, 80**).

Dudley subsequently listed more than eighty cases in which he believed that Henry had acted extortionately by taking excessive bonds, and declared that it had been the King's expressed purpose 'to have many persons at his danger' (**29**). In the reaction that set in after Henry's death nearly two hundred recognisances were cancelled and in a quarter of the cases it was specifically stated that this was because they had been unjustly extorted. But it would be wrong to assume that the strict enforcement of prerogative rights was only a feature of Henry's closing years. In fact it was his avowed and consistent policy throughout his reign and formed an integral part of his programme of restoring the Crown's finances at the same time as he imposed order upon a lawless society. Dudley's account book shows that in the period 1504–08 he 'collected' nearly £220,000 for the King. However, only £30,000 of this enormous sum was in hard cash. The rest consisted of promises to pay, and these recognisances were duly listed in the King's books, ready to be put into effect if the debtor misbehaved himself (**29**). As a system of law enforcement it was crude, and when Henry VIII inherited the Crown he ostentatiously broke with it. But Henry VIII had the advantage of coming to a throne that was comparatively secure and to a country that was relatively well ordered. The hard, and often dirty, work of accomplishing this had been done by his father.

The Council in Star Chamber and the 1487 tribunal

It used to be taken for granted by English historians that the Council in Star Chamber – from which the Court of Star Chamber was to emerge in Henry VIII's reign – was Henry VII's principal weapon in enforcing law and order, but it is now clear that this was not the case. Henry used a whole range of instruments and methods, of which some, such as the Council Learned and bonds and recognisances, have already been mentioned. The Council had a part to play in this process, but it was not a leading part. Sometimes, acting upon information received, it would take the initiative and either issue an executive order or summon the persons involved to appear before it [**doc. 6**]. In most instances, however, it acted like any other court and waited for a plaintiff to lodge a formal complaint. The records have survived of some three hundred cases considered by the Council, of which the majority were initiated by private suitors and were concerned with rioting. Yet even this is misleading, for an accusation of rioting was often little more than a legal fiction to cover what was really a dispute over land-ownership (**41, 42, 75**). A statute of Edward III's reign had forbidden the Council to deal with cases involving freehold, but by asserting that a riot had taken place a plaintiff could bring his accusation within the Council's competence. Why should he bother to do so when he could just as easily seek a remedy at common law? There were several reasons. For one thing the common law system was not functioning very efficiently (see below, p. 33). And, for another, the Council consisted of the most important men in the kingdom. Even if it merely remitted his case for consideration by a common law court the plaintiff might well have succeeded in speeding up the judicial process. Henry may initially have hoped, and even assumed, that his Council would take the lead in imposing order on a turbulent society but the revival and extension of conciliar jurisdiction merely swamped the hard-pressed Council with civil actions that could best have been dealt with elsewhere, and complicated rather than resolved Henry's problems: hence his resort to the more direct methods of bonds and recognisances (**96**).

The most obvious threats to order came from the widespread incidence of livery, maintenance and embracery [**doc. 9**], and if Henry's Council had concentrated its judicial activity on suppressing these it would have achieved something of real value. But it was limited by the fact that it could not inflict penalties involving the loss of life or limb, and for this reason it tended to leave such matters to the tribunal set up by the so-called Star Chamber Act of 1487 [**doc. 7**]. This tribunal consisted of the three chief members of Henry's Council, namely the Chancellor, Treasurer and Keeper of the Privy Seal, assisted by two other Councillors, one lay and one clerical, and the two Chief Justices. It was specifically empowered by the statute to enforce the laws relating to 'unlawful maintenances, giving of liveries, signs and tokens, and retainers . . . embraceries of his [the King's] subjects, untrue demeanings of sheriffs in making of panels [of jurors] and other untrue returns . . . taking of money by juries [and] great riots and unlawful assemblies'.

It seems likely that the 1487 tribunal was intended to play an important role in the task of bringing English society to heel, yet the records survive of only ten cases that were brought before it [**doc. 8**]. There may well have been others, and the fact that the 1487 statute was re-enacted in 1529 suggests that it had proved useful (**55, 75, 91**). But it cannot be emphasised too strongly that in Henry VII's reign there was no single or simple solution to the problem of restoring order. Henry's approach was essentially pragmatic. He tried a number of ways of achieving his aims, and concentrated on those that seemed to be succeeding. This undoubtedly led to overlapping and confusion, but to the extent that English society was more law-abiding in 1509 than it had been in 1485 Henry's method may be said to have worked.

Other Councils

The cost of bringing an action at common law effectively ruled out such a remedy for poor men. Under Edward IV the Council had, for this reason, appointed a second clerk, with responsibility for the 'custody, registration, and expedition of bills, requests and supplications of poor persons', and Richard III's reign saw the setting up of a regular tribunal for poor men's causes. This 'Court of Requests' lapsed in 1485, but during the latter part of Henry VII's reign poor men's causes were once again given special consideration, this time by a group of lesser Councillors consisting of clerics trained in civil and canon law as well as a number of common lawyers (**42, 75**). Not all those who brought their complaints to the attention of this conciliar tribunal were poor men by any means, but it is impossible, as always, to say why it, rather than the Council as a whole, should have taken cognisance of any particular case. The personnel of this tribunal probably fluctuated to some extent, and it never became totally detached from its parent body, the Council. Nevertheless it was already, in embryo, the Court of Requests for Poor Men's Causes that was to maintain an independent existence from Henry VIII's reign onwards.

The Council of the North was another institution which could trace its origins to the Yorkist period, though unlike the Court of Requests it was not an aspect or committee of the Council but had a separate existence from the very beginning. The north of England was a week's journey from London, and the border area with Scotland was lawless and undisciplined. The actual frontier zone was divided into three marches, each with a warden who was responsible for its defence. The east and middle marches were effectively under the control of the Percies, Earls of Northumberland, but their influence was challenged, in Edward IV's reign, by Richard, Duke of Gloucester, who inherited most of the Neville lands and became a northern magnate in his own right. Edward IV appointed Richard lieutenant of the north in 1482, and Richard's household council now became the administrative centre of the region, except for the eastern part where Northumberland maintained his influence.

Richard's rule in the north was popular, and when he became King he appointed his nephew, the Earl of Lincoln, to govern Yorkshire, and equipped him with a council which had authority 'to order and direct all riots, forcible entries . . . and other misbehaviours against our laws and peace committed and done in the said parts; and if such be that they in no wise can thoroughly order, then to refer it unto us and thereof certify us in all goodly haste thereafter'. This was the model on which the Tudor Council of the North was to be based in Henry VIII's reign.

Richard left control of the east and middle marches, and in effect of the whole frontier zone, in the hands of the fourth Earl of Northumberland. This arrangement was not to the liking of Henry VII, who distrusted the Percies both for their Yorkist sympathies and their princely power. He reluctantly appointed the earl as his lieutenant in the north, since there was no one else of equal stature available, but he was looking for an opportunity to supplant Percy influence in the border area by that of the Crown. His chance came in 1489, when Northumberland was killed in a riot at Thirsk while acting as the King's tax-collector (**89**). The earl's heir was a minor, and therefore became a royal ward, so Henry was able to assume the guardianship of his estates and take up the traditional Percy role as effective ruler of the marches (**48**).

Henry appointed Thomas Howard, Earl of Surrey, to act as his lieutenant in the north, though Surrey's rule was confined in practice to Yorkshire. Subsequently Henry nominated his eldest son, Prince Arthur, as Warden-General of the Marches, with Surrey as his under-warden. Royal officials, trained in Chamber organisation, were appointed both to the Prince's council and to that which Surrey had as the King's lieutenant. Most important of the officials on Surrey's council was William Sever, then an abbot but later Bishop of Carlisle, who was an expert in financial administration and kept in close touch with Bray in London. Sever's duties were to enforce prerogative rights in the north, and his powers – which were the usual mixture of administrative and judicial – were similar to those formally conferred in Henry VIII's reign on the President of the newly constituted Council of the North (**8, 27**).

The Welsh marches – the border area between Wales and England – were another disturbed region, partly because of the nature of the country and its people, and partly because of their distance from London in an age of poor communications. Edward IV, who, as Earl of March, was a marcher lord in his own right, conferred the principality of Wales on his baby son, Edward, in 1471, and appointed a council to manage it for him. The primary function of this council was the management of the Prince's estates, but in 1473 the King extended its authority to the marches, with instructions to restore and maintain order there. This, in the words of Penry

Williams, 'was the first stage in the process of turning the Prince's council from a body for administering estates into a court for enforcing the law' (**65** p. 7).

Henry VII, who added a number of marcher lordships to those which he acquired with the Crown, created his eldest son, Arthur, Prince of Wales in 1490, and three years later conferred on him virtually all the marcher lordships in the Crown's possession, including that of March. The Prince was sent to Ludlow, as a convenient seat from which to exercise his authority in Wales and the marcher area, and he almost certainly had a council to act for him, even though there is no record of its formal appointment until 1501. Arthur died in 1502, but the council continued in existence during the brief interregnum until the creation of Prince Henry as Prince of Wales in 1503. There were no further developments in the council during Henry VII's reign, but in 1504 the King inaugurated the practice of binding the marcher lords by indentures to maintain order. 'As far as a written and sealed undertaking, with a financial penalty clause, could do so, the Crown had established a machinery for order and justice in Wales: the Prince's council . . . was specifically required to superintend its working' (**30** p. 164).

The common law and Chancery

The common law was the ancient and customary law of England which had never been codified or written down but had been given coherence and some degree of definition by the decisions of royal judges over the course of several centuries. The more important of their judgements were recorded in the Year Books and acted as precedents to guide, but not necessarily to bind, their successors. Students acquired their knowledge of the common law through residence at one of the teaching institutions known as the Inns of Court, which were clustered near the Thames, midway between Westminster and the city of London. At any given time there were probably some two to three hundred students at the Inns of Court, though not all of them intended to become lawyers (**91**). Given the disturbed conditions of English society in the middle and late fifteenth century, and the frequent recourse to law to settle disputes about property, landowners needed to have a basic knowledge of the law, and they therefore sent their sons in increasing numbers to study at what was in effect the third university of the kingdom.

Those students who did complete their course and went on to become professional lawyers might form part of the group of some four hundred people who were involved in the running of the central courts at Westminster, of which the most important were King's Bench and Common Pleas. Each of these courts was presided over by a Chief Justice, assisted by a number of lesser or puisne judges, and they held their sessions in the great hall at Westminster which William Rufus had built. They sat during the four legal terms only, and since each of these occupied no more than three weeks it meant that justice could be done for a mere three months a year. This limited provision was further restricted by the fact that the judges sat for only three hours each day, and that proceedings were conducted in Norman French – a bastard dialect which, by Henry VII's time, was incomprehensible to anyone outside the legal profession. However, twice a year the judges of the central courts set out on the assizes which took them to the principal cities of the kingdom, where they were received with all the dignity and deference appropriate to the King's representatives, and dealt with cases remitted to them by the local Justices of the Peace.

The law was a profession which was highly thought of and could bring rich rewards. Not all lawyers practised in London. Many found employment in manorial or church courts or as clerks to JPs. And of those who stayed in London a significant proportion went into the service of the King. This was particularly marked during the reign of Edward IV, who created the new office of Solicitor-General to supplement that of Attorney-General which had been instituted under Henry VI. About a third of all the non-noble members of Edward's Council were lawyers, and the proportion was even greater under Henry VII. From 1484 until the middle of the sixteenth century all the Speakers of the House of Commons were lawyers, and of ten Chancellors of the Duchy of Lancaster appointed between 1471 and 1529 seven had a legal training (**91**).

If a plaintiff wished to begin an action before King's Bench or Common Pleas he had first to purchase a writ. In theory the forms of writ were limited to those which had obtained in Edward I's day, but in practice, and largely through the use of legal fictions, there was considerable flexibility (**20**). However, a minor inaccuracy in a writ could invalidate the whole case, and defence lawyers were skilled in the use of technicalities to delay proceedings. As a consequence cases could drag on. Even the simplest was likely to take eighteen months, and the more complicated ones might last for several years (**52**). In assize courts and quarter sessions a trial was usually initiated through presentment by a grand jury, consisting of the more substantial inhabitants of the locality. The idea was that such men were likely to be acquainted with the accused person and know whether the charges against him were well founded. Only if they approved of the bill of indictment would the case go ahead.

However, the indictment of an offender did not automatically mean that he was brought to trial. He had first to be apprehended, and this was not always easy. There was no police force, and the parish constable was more often than not a figure of fun. Even when offenders were pursued by the sheriff and his officers they could claim sanctuary in parish churches, churchyards, and a large number of other places. In the unlikely event of their being actually arrested they still had a good chance of escaping trial. Those who could read had the right to claim benefit of clergy (see below, p. 56); others might be released on the grounds that the indictment against them contained a technical inaccuracy, such as the misspelling of a name. Assuming that a case came to trial, there was no certainty that it would reach a satisfactory conclusion. Twelve men would be chosen by the sheriff to form the trial jury, but they, even more than the grand jurymen (who were drawn from a somewhat higher social level) were susceptible to bribery, intimidation or blackmail from interested parties. Even if they found the accused guilty there was only a small chance that he would undergo the prescribed punishment. All too frequently he would simply disappear, and although the courts could resort to an ascending hierarchy of fulminations, culminating in a declaration of outlawry, these were rarely effective. Indeed, one of the reasons why Henry VII created the office of Surveyor of the King's Prerogative (see above, p. 20) was to improve the procedures for rounding up outlaws and thereby restore confidence in the ability of the common law courts to do justice.

Henry also tried to check the abuse of the jury system, through two statutes passed by the 1495 parliament. The first of these required Justices of the Peace to watch over the sheriff when he empanelled juries [**doc. 9**], while the second authorised them to dispense with juries of presentment in certain cases. It may be doubted whether either of these statutes achieved its purpose, for the facts of life in early Tudor England were such that local magnates were far better placed to get their way – even if this involved perverting the course of justice – than the agents of the distant King. Magnate power derived in large part from the practice of retaining, for a lord with liveried retainers in his service had, in the words of one of Henry VII's judges, 'a great company at his command. And for this [reason] men do not dare to execute the law on any of them' (**36** p. 92). There was already in existence a statute of 1468 forbidding the retaining of anyone except menial servants, but this did not, in practice, apply to peers, who were likely to be the worst offenders [**doc. 10**]. In November 1485 the members of Henry VII's first parliament, Commons as well as Lords, swore the oath prescribed under the 1468 statute by which they bound themselves not to 'retain any man by indenture or oath, or give livery, sign or token contrary to the law'. The value of such a promise, however solemnly affirmed, was limited, as Sir William Hussey, Chief Justice of the King's Bench, made plain, for he recalled how a similar ceremony had taken place in Edward IV's reign, yet 'he saw, within an hour, while they were in the Star Chamber, divers of the lords make retainments by oath and surety and other things which were directly contrary to their said sureties and oaths; and so oaths and sureties are to no purpose' (**36** p. 91).

Henry VII never attempted to forbid retaining altogether. Even if such a step had been practicable it would have been unwise, for in the absence of any police force or standing army the King depended upon his greater subjects for the maintenance of public order, and they could only act effectively because they had private armies of retainers at their disposal. The effectiveness (or otherwise) of retaining as a law-enforcement mechanism depended upon the attitude of the individual who did the retaining and also upon his relationship with the King. If he chose to employ his potential strength in a responsible manner he could impose discipline upon his local community. If not, he would usually be able to ride roughshod over judicial institutions and legal procedures and get his way by brute force. The King was prepared to tolerate a considerable degree of self help of this sort if it worked in his favour, and he encouraged retaining where it was to his advantage to do so – as in the case of his trusted servant Sir Thomas Lovell, whom he appointed Keeper of Sherwood Forest and Constable of Nottingham Castle, thereby enabling him to retain some 1,400 men for his own, and the Crown's, service.

The only peer who was brought before a common law court on a charge of retaining in Henry VII's reign was George Neville, Lord Burgavenny. He held considerable estates in Kent, but had come under suspicion for his failure to act effectively against the Cornish rebels when they were marching towards London in 1497. It was not until ten years later, however, that he was indicted before King's Bench on a charge of retaining 471 men for thirty months and binding them 'to do both on foot and on horse, lawfully and unlawfully', whatever he commanded (**36**). The court found him guilty and subjected him to the penalty prescribed in the 1468 statute – namely 100 shillings for each month for which each man was unlawfully retained. This meant a total fine of well over £70,000 and the only question that remained to be decided was how much of it Henry would collect, and under what conditions. In fact Henry added to Burgavenny's financial burden by making him give recognisances for good behaviour [**doc. 4**]. The unfortunate peer eventually had to acknowledge that he was indebted to Henry in the sum of £100,000, but the King, 'of his most gracious and merciful disposition', condescended to accept a mere £50,000, to be paid in ten annual instalments. However it was specifically provided that 'all the residue of the said sum of £100,000 was to be at all times by our said sovereign lord, at his most gracious and high pleasure, demandable and leviable'.

By the time Burgavenny was brought to trial Henry had reinforced the royal authority by the statute of 1504 which required all those who had retainers to submit a list of their names to the King and obtain a licence from him [**doc. 11**]. This was the first occasion on which the nobles' right to retain men for their service had been called in question, and it marked a big step forward in establishing the principle that retaining should henceforth only be legal if it operated in the public interest. There was no sudden transformation, of course, and disorder, for which retaining was in large part responsible, continued to be a problem for Henry's successors. Yet his efforts to set bounds on retaining had some measure of success even within his own lifetime, and he established the principle which later Tudors put into practice.

Although the common law had as its primary function the protection of property, more and more property cases were going to the court of Chancery in the late fifteenth century. This was because Chancery, unlike Common Pleas, took cognisance of trusts or 'uses', and also of commercial transactions. In the closing years of Henry VI's reign Chancery had handled some 140 cases a year, compared with just under 80 for the Exchequer, 1,600 for King's Bench, and 13,500 for Common Pleas. Under Edward IV this figure rose to 550, and by the time Henry VII died Chancery was dealing with some 600 cases a year. In the words of the court's historian, 'It is clear that it was during the Yorkist period that Chancery changed from an administrative department with a certain amount of judicial business to becoming one of the four central courts of the realm' (**55** p. 39). It was still much smaller than King's Bench or Common Pleas, of course, even though the number of cases coming before these two courts had fallen sharply as a result of the disturbed conditions which marked the late-Lancastrian period and also the decreasing effectiveness of their procedures. The growing importance of Chancery was in part a reflection of the changing position of the Lord Chancellor, who was now emerging as the King's chief minister and the most powerful figure in the royal administration. As such he commanded an authority which could not be matched by the Chief Justices of King's Bench or Common Pleas.

Although landowners were turning to Chancery in increasing numbers to sort out their difficulties, the basic cause for the big rise in the quantity of cases coming before the court was the need of the urban communities to find solutions in law for the financial and commercial disputes in which they were frequently and inevitably involved. From the point of view of the court, however, the source of litigation was largely irrelevant. What it had to take into account was the fact that it was being called upon to give a legal remedy in disputes that were often highly intricate, and this demanded a different type of expertise from that to which it was accustomed. Until the mid-fifteenth century Chancery had been largely staffed by clerics with a training in theology, but Morton's appointment as Master of the Rolls in 1472 marks a watershed, for he was a Doctor of Civil Law, and from then onwards the personnel of Chancery was drawn mainly from graduates in civil law, many of them straight down from university. Their professionalism further increased the effectiveness, and therefore the popularity, of the court (**55**).

Justices of the Peace

Sir William Hussey, speaking to his fellow judges in the first year of Henry VII's reign, declared that 'The laws will never be well executed until all the lords spiritual and temporal are of one accord to execute them effectually, and when the King on his part and the lords on their part both want to do this and do it' (**30** p. 77). There could be no doubt about the King's desire to see the laws put into execution, but where law-enforcement was concerned he was dependent to a considerable extent upon the Justices of the Peace. These officers were appointed annually from among the leading gentry of every shire, and were charged by the Commission of the Peace with the responsibility for maintaining order in their localities. Their duties were substantially increased by statute during the Tudor period, and Henry VII's reign saw an Act of 1487 giving them authority to take bail, and the one of 1495, already mentioned, making it lawful for them to act upon information received without waiting for formal indictment by a grand jury.

Much of the Justices' work in any shire was done by a handful of them sitting together as the needs of their situation and their own convenience dictated. But four times a year formal Quarter Sessions were held, at which all the Justices were supposed to be present and which were also attended by most people of consequence in the shire. At these Quarter Sessions the JPs tried all those indicted of any crime except treason – which was always investigated by the Council – and either passed sentence themselves, or, in difficult cases, left the accused to be dealt with by the assize judges.

The JPs were not simply judicial officers. They were also responsible for supervising the administration of their shires, and at Quarter Sessions they enquired into the conduct of all local officials, including mayors and sheriffs. Parliament added to their duties in this respect, as by an Act of 1495 which required them to suppress unlawful games and to control ale-houses. The regulation of economic activity, which had previously been the concern of the manorial courts or of the old popular courts of the shire and hundred, was also being taken over by the JPs, and here again Parliament increased their range of duties. In 1504, to give one example, they were made responsible for seeing that pewter and brass were of the prescribed degree of fineness.

Henry could rely upon the Justices' own self-interest as property owners for the maintenance of peace and good order, and he could always use the threat of removal from the Commission of the Peace – though he might have problems in finding a replacement, for the number of men of substance in any shire was quite small. Delinquent JPs could be summoned before Chancery or the common law courts, and King's Bench could annul decisions taken at Quarter Sessions if it thought the Justices had failed to carry out their duties in a responsible and impartial manner. A statute of 1489 required JPs to read out a proclamation at Quarter Sessions clearly defining their powers, and it made provision for anyone with a grievance to take his complaint either to the assize judges or direct to the

King. Such primitive and clumsy machinery was not, however, very effective, and the Act should be regarded more as an expression of intent than an actual remedy.

Paid royal officials, dependent for their living upon the King's goodwill, would have been far more useful from Henry's point of view and he was said to have expressed a desire 'to govern England in the French fashion' (**5** p. 178). But as Henry himself recognised, he could not do so. A corps of royal officials would have cost far more than the Crown had available, and in any case Henry had acquired, along with the Crown, a system of local administration which, whatever its weaknesses, worked quite well, could be made to work better, and cost virtually nothing. Government on the cheap, in the localities as well as at the centre, was to remain one of the characteristics of Tudor England, but the Tudor sovereigns had to pay a price for it in terms of power. They could impose their authority only up to a certain point. Beyond that they needed the co-operation of the political nation.

If the King was dependent upon the Justices of the Peace, the Justices themselves were dependent upon the lesser officials charged with bringing offenders to book. Every hundred was bound by law to provide itself with a high constable, and every parish with a petty constable, and these appointments were usually made by the JPs. Such offices were highly unpopular, since the remuneration was insignificant and the risks attached to the performance of their duties were considerable. The constables were spare-time officials, who could rely only on themselves. There were few volunteers for such posts, and the JPs frequently had to use their powers of compulsion in order to fill them. The consequence was that at the lowest levels of society, where the forces of law and order came into closest and most direct contact with the forces of disorder, there was a lack of will and means, and a great deal of crime went unpunished.

In cases of riot or rebellion the King could call out armed forces, but here again a shortage of money, as well as the prevailing antipathy towards the idea of a standing army, left the sovereign dependent upon the co-operation of his greater subjects. Henry had a small force of Yeomen of the Guard as well as a handful of mercenaries at his disposal [**doc. 12**]. He also had, at Calais, a garrison of some 800 men, which was considered enormous and cost £10,000 a year to maintain – though, fortunately for Henry, this charge was borne directly by the Company of the Staple. Whenever troops

were needed on a large scale Henry had to send out Commissions
of Array to the leading men in every county, ordering them to levy
men for his service. In its military, as in its financial resources,
then, the Tudor monarchy stood on very narrow foundations.

7 Parliament

In Henry VII's England government was essentially a matter for the King and his Council. Parliament was neither an integral nor a regular part of this machinery. The King called it as and when he wished, and Henry claimed credit for the fact that his parliaments were infrequent and that his subjects were thereby saved the expense of paying for their representatives to make constant visits to Westminster. Henry reigned for twenty-four years, but during this time he met only seven parliaments, of which five took place in the first ten years of the reign. All but three of Henry's parliaments met for one session only, lasting a few weeks at most, and second sessions, when they did take place, were as short-lived as first ones. The total time taken up by meetings in the period from 1485 to 1509 was sixty-nine weeks – just under three weeks for each year of the reign – yet even this figure tends to exaggerate their importance, since from 1497 to 1509 there were only two parliaments, which between them lasted for about 120 days: this gives an average for the last thirteen years of Henry's reign of just over nine days a year.

The Lords

Parliament was still primarily what it had been in the Middle Ages, a meeting of the King and his Councillors with the peers of the realm. The Commons took little direct part, and were technically onlookers at the main proceedings. The Lords met in a room in the royal palace at Westminster, where they were grouped around the throne. The King himself frequently presided at meetings, and when he was absent his place was taken by the Lord Chancellor. Near the throne sat the judges and other members of the Council, but they were there as advisers, and took no part in debates or voting. It was because non-noble Councillors were unable to play a full part in proceedings of the Lords that many of them preferred to stand for election to the so-called Lower House – a sign that the centre of political power was gradually shifting.

The Lords consisted of two estates, the spiritual and the secular. Only thirteen archbishops and bishops and seventeen abbots and priors came to the first parliament of Henry's reign, but in a full house the spiritual peers totalled just under fifty. The lay lords were much fewer in number, and only eighteen were present at Henry's first parliament. This was partly because of attainders, but was primarily due to the fact that the heads of many noble houses were minors – the result of natural causes, intensified by the Wars of the Roses. As the reign progressed, minors came of age, attainders were reversed, and dormant titles were revived, until there were about forty lords temporal available for meetings of parliament. Even if they had all attended they would still have been in a minority, but the number present for any parliamentary session is not known. It could well be that in practice the Upper House was not much more than a slightly enlarged meeting of the royal Council (**29, 52**). This Council was itself the descendant, at many removes, of the medieval *magnum concilium*, in which the magnates had met the King to discuss important matters and tender their advice. The shadow of this still survived, in the shape of assemblies of peers at which the King and his Councillors were present but no representatives of the Commons. There were about five or six of these *magna concilia* during Henry's reign, but they were of limited utility. The *magnum concilium*, in fact, was turning into the House of Lords – although this term did not become current until Henry VIII's reign – and parliament was much more of a partnership between Lords and Commons than the formally inferior position of the Lower House suggested. This was indicated by a change in the procedure for dealing with bills that took place in Henry VII's reign. At Henry's accession it was still the practice for public bills to be introduced first into the Lords, and then, when they were sent down for discussion by the Commons, to take precedence over bills that had originated in the Lower House. This practice was still current in the 1497 parliament, but not in that of 1504. 'Procedurally speaking' then, as G. R. Elton observes, 'the parliament of 1497 was the last medieval parliament' (**82** p. 54).

Elton also points out that although Henry VII continued his predecessors' practice of amending bills after they had completed their passage through both Houses, he did not do so with 'the lavish abandonment of Edward IV'. Furthermore he was the last King to exercise this right. By the end of his reign it was no longer a question of the Lower House presenting, in the form of bills, what were really petitions, which the King could modify as he thought fit, even though the Lords had approved of them. From 1504 onwards the Lords and Commons were working closely together – often, of course, with guidance from royal Councillors – to produce what were in effect re-statements of the law. These had to be carefully drafted, for since Richard III's reign it had been the practice for statutes to be printed (**66**). They thereby gained a degree of determinateness and of authority which had been lacking in the days of handwritten copies.

The Commons

The Commons were already a House, both in fact and in current phraseology, by the time Henry VII came to the throne, since they had to be called something to distinguish them from the Lords, who in theory *were* parliament. While the Lords and the King discussed affairs of state in the royal palace, the Commons met in the nearby chapter-house of the abbey of Westminster. If Henry had anything of particular importance to say he might well summon the Commons to appear before him – as he did in his first parliament, in order to give them a lecture on his right to the throne. But strictly speaking the Commons took no part in meetings of parliament except at the opening and closing ceremonies, when they squeezed into cramped positions at one end of the room (technically outside it) in which the King and the Lords were seated, and made a report of their separate proceedings through the mouth of their Speaker.

The choice of Speaker was in theory made by the Commons themselves, who elected one of their own number, but by the time Henry VII ascended the throne the election was little more than a formality, and all the Speakers of the reign – of whom Thomas Lovell was the first – were royal nominees. Until 1544 the Speakers were chosen from among the knights of the shire, who had, as a group, a certain pre-eminence in the Lower House. Two knights were elected for each of the thirty-seven shires by freeholders who held land to the value of at least forty shillings (£2) a year, but the majority of members – 222 in Henry VII's reign – sat for boroughs, and were elected on a variety of franchises, in which the only common element was the importance of the merchant oligarchy which controlled most towns. Not all the burgesses in the House of Commons were townsmen. The process had already started by which local landowners put themselves forward as candidates for election to a borough seat, often holding out the inducement of paying their own expenses if they were elected, instead of demanding – as they

43

had a legal right to do – that the constituency should reimburse them. There was no reason why local gentry should not represent a borough's interests as effectively as townsmen, and by 1500 it may well be that as many as half the burgesses in the House were in fact gentry. Members of the royal Council would also stand for borough seats, since they could play a much more significant part in the proceedings of the Lower House than they could in those of the Upper.

Because they were part of the High Court of Parliament, whose work must not be impeded by the processes of any inferior courts, members of the Commons had certain privileges. They could not, for instance, be arrested for debt, breach of contract, or other civil suit, while parliament was in session. As for their discussions, if the Speaker misreported these they had the right – formally granted to them, in response to the Speaker's request, at the opening of every parliament – to amend his report [**doc. 13**]. From this limited privilege was to develop the great claim to freedom of speech, but no such claim was ever made by the Commons in Henry's reign. For one thing they stood in awe of the King, and would be no more likely to criticise him inside the House than outside. For another they approved, in general, of what Henry was doing, since the benefits of peace and good order were only too apparent to them. Short and infrequent sessions meant, in any case, that they had little time in which to develop a sense of corporate identity in opposition to the King. They were summoned for a specific purpose, namely to consent to what the King had decided, and the assumption – which they shared – was that they would consent.

Even if individual members felt strongly enough about particular matters to oppose a measure, they ran the risk of incurring the royal wrath. Henry was not, of course, a member of the House of Commons, but many of his Councillors were, and they acted as his eyes and ears. This is the significance of Roper's story that Thomas More, having been elected as a burgess to the parliament of 1504, dared to oppose a request for taxation, and 'made such arguments and reasons there against, that the King's demands were thereby overthrown. So that one of the King's Privy Chamber, named Mr. Tyler, being present thereat, brought word to the King out of the Parliament House, that a beardless boy had disappointed all his purposes. Whereupon the King, conceiving great indignation towards him, could not be satisfied until he had some way revenged it. And forasmuch as he, nothing having, nothing could lose, his grace devised a causeless quarrel against his father, keeping him in the Tower until he had paid him an hundred pounds fine'(**15** p. 7). If this story is true (see below, p. 48) – and it is worth remembering that Roper was More's son-in-law, and presumably heard it from More's own lips – it shows the sort of pressures that could be brought to bear on members of the Commons who dared oppose a measure decided on by the King.

Henry's success in controlling parliament may be judged by the fact that although he amended a number of bills he never needed to veto any. This was the result partly of careful management, but mainly of the identity of interest between the King and the property-owners whom he summoned to meet him. Lancastrian parliaments, and particularly the Commons, had pressed for the adoption of a reform programme designed to increase the efficiency of the Crown rather than impede it. Members now had a monarch who was putting that reform programme into effect, and not surprisingly they willingly co-operated with him. Political stability was a rare blessing in late fifteenth-century England, and it was not until towards the end of Henry VII's reign that the property-owners could begin to take it for granted and ask themselves whether they were paying too high a price.

The functions of parliament

1 MONEY GRANTS

From Henry's point of view one of the advantages of summoning representatives of the community to Westminster was that he could there address, as it were, the whole nation. Every parliament was a dialogue, in which the King could learn about the state of the localities, while the representatives of those localities could find out what measures of the government would affect them, and in what way. When members returned to their constituencies they were expected to act not simply as journalists, giving the news from the capital, but also as government propagandists – since, by their consent in parliament, they were committed to the support even of unpopular measures like taxes. They could also be used in a more direct fashion, as in 1495, when they were given new standards of weights and measures to distribute in their localities.

While parliament was useful as a means of two-way communication, it was essential for the granting of money and for the making of statute law. The first parliament of the reign, which met in 1485, granted Henry tunnage and poundage, on wool, woolfells and leather for the rest of his life [**doc. 14**]. This particular indirect tax had originally been intended for the defence of the kingdom, and the grant to Henry was made 'in especial for the safeguard and keeping of the sea', but in fact there was no check on how the King used the sums so obtained. The advantage of tunnage and poundage was that its value increased as trade flourished, and Henry's success in restoring ordered conditions and promoting commerce was directly rewarded by a larger income from this source.

In spite of the grant of tunnage and poundage, Henry was short of money in the early years of his reign. He had contracted debts as an exile which had to be repaid, and even after his accession he was forced to spend heavily on defending his position against pretenders. In 1486 and 1489 he sent commissioners into the counties to demand loans from his richer subjects [**doc. 15**] – loans which worked out, on the average, at £1 per head – and although this method of raising money seems crude to modern eyes, it was successful and apparently aroused little resentment. Henry's reputation was enhanced, and his credit improved, by the fact that these loans were apparently all repaid.

Henry, like Edward IV before him, aimed to 'live of his own' and not to trouble his subjects except in case of necessity; but war was generally regarded as justifying parliamentary taxation, and in 1487 parliament was summoned to provide money for the suppression of Simnel's rising. It voted two fifteenths and tenths – the first direct tax of the reign – as well as a graduated poll-tax on foreign traders. In theory fifteenths and tenths were levies on personal property, but since the reign of Edward III they had become increasingly stereotyped, and now represented a sum of a little under £30,000 made up by fixed contributions from every parish. The advantage of this was obvious from the point of view of those who voted the taxes. They knew exactly what they were committing themselves to, and they also profited from the fact that a standardised grant took no account of increased wealth; where, as had happened in many cases, the burden of taxation fell most heavily on those who were least able to afford it, the richer section of society could continue to enjoy its built-in benefit.

The Crown, on the other hand, felt the need for a more flexible system, and throughout the period of Lancastrian rule the Exchequer had tried a number of experiments designed to bring taxation into a closer relationship with real wealth. This attempt was renewed in 1489, when parliament voted £100,000 to help the King in his struggle to stop France from swallowing the duchy of Brittany (see below, p. 70). Three-quarters of this sum was to be raised by the laity, through an income tax of 10 per cent and a levy on personal property. The assessment was to be made by royal commissioners, sent into the counties for this specific purpose, but the novelty of the tax caused widespread disturbance, particularly among the poor, who regarded it as a device to squeeze yet more money out of them. Anger flared into rebellion in the north of England, where the Earl of Northumberland, acting – most uncharacteristically for a Percy – as a royal tax-collector, was killed in a brawl at Thirsk. The rebels went on to attack York, and Henry had to raise an army to restore order. Taxation levied at this cost was self-defeating, and parliament had to vote a conventional tenth and fifteenth to make up the deficit. But Henry was not prepared to abandon his attempts to get a more realistic and flexible method of tax assessment. He repeated the experiment in 1497 and 1504, and the fact that he raised more than £30,000 on each occasion suggests that he was gaining the acquiesence, if not the support, of the tax-payers, and thereby preparing the way for the directly-assessed, open-ended subsidy which was to become the standard form of taxation in Tudor England.[1]

In July 1491, when Anne of Brittany called on Henry for his support against France, the King demanded a 'Benevolence' from his richer subjects and corporations. A Benevolence – so-called because it was supposedly granted out of the *benevolentia* or goodwill of the giver – was regarded as a gift, not to be repaid. The main advantage of it from the King's point of view was speedy collection and the fact that, since it did not affect the poorer elements in society, it was not likely to lead to rioting [**doc. 16**]. It might be thought that those who paid the Benevolence would have resented it, but the 1495 parliament gave it implicit approval by authorising Henry to collect any sums outstanding. It may be that members recognised the justice of Henry's claim that they, having more, should contribute more; or perhaps they calculated that if they co-operated

---

[1] The figures given here are based on an unpublished Ph.D thesis (1963) by R. S. Schofield, 'Parliamentary Lay Taxation 1485–1547', in the Cambridge University Library. According to this, the yields for Henry VII's reign were as follows:

Lay Subsidies				*Fifteenths and Tenths*	
1488	£571	1488	£29,072	1492(II)	£27,011
1489	£18,300	1489	£29,405	1497(I)	£29,266
1497	£30,088	1490–91	£28,861	1497(II)	£29,252
1504	£30,873	1492(I)	£29,300		

with the King in this respect, he would not be driven to fleece them in other ways.

Parliament's general approval of Henry's foreign policy was demonstrated in October 1491, when two fifteenths and tenths were voted, with the promise of a third if the English army had to spend a long time campaigning on the continent [**doc. 17**]. Five years later Henry needed money to protect his kingdom against the Scots, and decided to demand a loan. He first summoned a *magnum concilium*, to which certain burgesses and merchants were also invited. This hybrid body 'granted' the King £120,000, and with this demonstration of support to aid them the royal commissioners were able to raise loans amounting to just under half that sum. In January of the following year, 1497, a full parliament assembled, and voted two fifteenths and tenths to cover the King's past expenses, and a further 'aid and subsidy of as great and large sums of money as the said two fifteenths and tenths . . . should have amounted to'. This was heavy taxation by the standards of early-Tudor England, and it drove the Cornishmen – who could not see why they should have to pay hard-earned money for the defence of far-distant and alien northerners – into revolt (see below, p. 74).

Henry made only one more demand for direct taxation after this date. In 1504 he asked parliament to authorise the payment of two feudal aids, one for the knighting of his eldest son, the other for the marriage of his eldest daughter. The legality of such demands could not be contested, even though Prince Arthur had been knighted fifteen years earlier and was now dead, while the marriage of Princess Margaret to the King of Scotland had taken place in the previous year. However, the members of parliament feared that the demand for a feudal aid was merely a pretext for an investigation into the nature of landholding throughout England, which might well increase their liability to wardship and other hated feudal incidents. This was no doubt Henry's intention: hence his anger when young Thomas More persuaded the Commons to reject his proposal (see above, p. 45). In the end the Commons offered a subsidy of £40,000, of which the King was graciously pleased to remit a quarter.

Apart from this incident in 1504 Henry had little trouble with parliament where money was concerned. In fact he raised well over a quarter of a million pounds through parliamentary taxation, most of it in the first decade of his reign. If clerical taxation is taken into account, along with the Benevolence of 1491, it becomes apparent that Henry's subjects contributed an average of almost £14,000 a year to the royal revenues.

2 LAW-MAKING

If parliament's existence had depended solely upon its exclusive right to vote taxes it would have ended after the first ten years or so of Henry's reign, by which time the King was not simply out of debt but beginning to accumulate a reserve of treasure. However, parliament had one other important function which it alone could perform – namely, the making of statute law. It is true, of course, that Henry made extensive use of proclamations to enforce his will, but although (in the words of R. W. Heinze) he 'obviously considered royal proclamations a useful and necessary instrument of governing . . . he never used them in a way that posed any threat to parliament' (**45** p. 84).

Statute was the highest form of law and had the enormous advantage that, unlike proclamations, it was enforceable in the courts of common law. In the late fifteenth and early sixteenth centuries there was increasing emphasis throughout Europe upon the rights of the ruler and the duty of subjects to obey, yet in England it remained a fact that the King's powers were limited by the common law. Although he appointed the judges, who held office only during his pleasure, and although he could insist that when any case directly concerned him he should be consulted before action was taken, he could not change the law which the judges and courts administered unless he first obtained the consent of the Lords and Commons in parliament.

Henry made considerable use of statutes to carry out his policies. There were just under two hundred public Acts passed during his reign, and the average number per session was about the same as under Henry VIII. Many government measures made their first appearance in the Commons, for although members' first concern was with private bills which they promoted for the benefit of their particular constituencies, the House would put forward public bills on matters of general interest. The government would sometimes take over a Commons' initiative, and it would also introduce measures of its own where it saw a need. It is not always possible to distinguish between government proposals and those which sprang from the Commons, but there is no evidence to suggest that the government was anxious to diminish the Commons' role. The Commons had an obvious interest in social and economic measures, and it may well be that many of the penal statutes from which Henry profited (by collecting fines for infringement of them) were the result of pressure from the Lower House rather than cunning schemes devised by the King for his own enrichment.

One of the major functions of parliament was the strengthening of the Crown, and the first parliament of Henry's reign declared, for the 'avoiding of all ambiguities and questions', that 'the inheritance of the crowns of the realms of England and of France, with all the pre-eminence and dignity royal to the same pertaining, and all other seignories to the King belonging beyond the sea . . . be, rest, remain and abide in the most royal person of our now sovereign lord King Harry the VIIth and in the heirs of his body lawfully coming' [**doc. 18**]. There was no question, of course, of Henry seeking a 'parliamentary title' to the Crown, which he claimed by right of descent. The object of the statute was simply to ensure that Henry's authority could not be challenged in the courts, and that he should have full possession of all royal lands. The 'De Facto' Act of 1495 was another measure designed to strengthen the Crown by encouraging men to serve it wholeheartedly, without constantly looking over their shoulders to see whether a pretender was on the horizon.

There was one further way in which parliament reinforced Henry's position. This was through striking down his enemies by Acts of attainder, which transferred their property to the Crown [**doc. 19**]. Acts of attainder had been used frequently during the Wars of the Roses to cripple adherents of the defeated side, and Henry opened his reign with a batch of attainders against prominent Yorkists. The second parliament of the reign saw twenty-eight attainders, following the suppression of the Simnel conspiracy, and Henry kept up this heavy pressure upon his opponents even after he had become firmly established on the throne. His last parliament, in 1504, passed more Acts of attainder than any of the others, and only the parliament of 1497 was entirely free of them.

Parliament was concerned not only with reinforcing Henry's hold on the throne but also with restoring order to a disturbed country. This accounts for the fact that over ten per cent of the statutes passed during the reign dealt with the duties of Justices of the Peace. In 1485 an Act empowered them to issue a warrant for the arrest of any person and to carry out a preliminary examination of him on suspicion alone, without waiting for formal indictment by a grand jury; and in 1495 came the Act already mentioned, authorising JPs to hear and determine, without indictment, all offences short of felony. They were also required to supervise and control local officials and to amend jury panels chosen by the sheriff if the latter had failed to act impartially [**doc. 9**].

Parliament was also used by Henry to bring corporations and franchises more closely under his control. Statutes were passed regulating the town governments of Northampton and Leicester; and in 1495 the franchise of Tynedale was annexed to the shire administration. Even a great and proud corporation like London was brought to heel. In 1487 a statute annulled the City ordinances forbidding citizens to take their goods to fairs and markets outside London and ten years later parliament stepped in to stop the Merchant Adventurers of London from monopolising the valuable cloth trade of the country by imposing a high entrance fee for membership of their company (see below, p. 61). This was followed by an Act of 1504 in which it was laid down that 'no masters, wardens and fellowships of crafts . . . nor any rulers of gilds or fraternities, take upon them to make any acts or ordinances . . . but if the same acts or ordinances be examined and approved by the Chancellor, Treasurer of England, and Chief Justices of either Bench'. Henry in fact had little trouble with corporations, but these statutes emphasised the principle that all jurisdictional and legislative rights derived from the Crown, and could, if necessary, be controlled or even resumed.

The principle of centralisation was also applied by parliament in matters which affected the country's economy, since local variations in standards hindered trade. Acts were passed to improve the coinage and to establish uniform weights and measures, and members were urged to see that these were carried into effect. Attempts were also made to limit the effects of economic change. In 1489, for instance, came the first general statute against depopulation and eviction; and in 1485 and 1489 Navigation Acts were passed, with the aim of promoting the shipping industry, and through it the navy (see below, p. 65).

Further measures were concerned with social discipline, such as the Act of 1495 which laid down maximum wage rates and minimum hours of work, and forbade the withholding of labour. Another Act of this year ordered that vagabonds found in towns should be put in the stocks and then expelled, while beggars were to be returned to their original place of residence. Behind much of this legislation may be discerned fear – fear that labourers might combine to demand higher wages and shorter hours of work; fear that the unemployed might accumulate in the towns, providing fod-

der for rebellion. Fear may also be discerned behind a number of
statutes for licensing trade and imposing certain standards. In these
cases the fear was that if the operation of the economy was left
entirely alone, some trades and industries would attract too many
participants, thereby reducing the level of profit and encouraging
unscrupulous men to defraud customers by lowering the quality of
their goods. The statutes concerned with licensing were usually
'penal' – that is, they encouraged the use of informers, and provided that in the case of a successful prosecution the penalty should
be shared between the informer and the King.

Parliament's concern for social discipline led it into the frontier
land between church and state, with the Act of 1489 limiting benefit
of clergy (see below, p. 56). The justification for this legislation,
however, was that it concerned law and order, and parliament
made no attempt in the reign of the first Tudor to trespass into the
field of spiritual matters. Although in some ways it acted as a
supreme lawgiver it also recognised implicit limitations upon its
freedom of action. The big extension of parliamentary competence
did not come until after 1529.

8 The Church

There were some nine thousand parishes in England, but at any one time a quarter of these were likely to be without a resident incumbent. This was not because of any shortage of clergy, for there may have been as many as 30,000 priests, as well as hundreds of men in minor orders. Non-residence was usually the result of pluralism, for if a minister held more than one living he could clearly not be resident in all of them. The roots of pluralism went deep into the structure of the Church of England, for the *Ecclesia Anglicana* was the largest single organisation in the country and it needed a considerable bureaucracy to enable it to function. Clerical bureaucrats were therefore appointed to one or more parishes on the understanding that while they would draw the tithes they would not be resident or perform any pastoral functions. These would be carried out instead by a curate, to whom they would pay a small stipend (**44, 52**).

This system was not without its merits. It was better for the Church to be run by clerics rather than lay administrators, and there was no reason why a curate should not be as committed or effective as an incumbent. But as the historian of the diocese of Lincoln has pointed out, there was another side to the picture. 'From the point of view of the parish, tithe paid to a non-resident was so much money down the drain. The curate or priest in charge of livings which supported non-resident incumbents would have felt much the same way. Few of them received more than £5 for doing all the work in the parish; they were often paid less than a quarter of the real value of the living' (**25** p. 103).

It was generally reckoned that an income of £15 a year was sufficient for a parish priest to fulfil his obligations without being overburdened with financial worries, but only about one in four parishes produced as much as this. In half, the income of the incumbent was under £10. It would have made economic sense to amalgamate the poorer livings, but in practice it was the richer ones which were subject to pluralism, since this was the easiest way of providing an adequate income for a clerical bureaucrat. The irony of the situation was that the Church had succeeded in raising the educational level of its clergy, but had not thereby benefited the parishes. University-trained clerics, usually with a degree in civil or canon law, were all too frequently snapped up either by bishops, who needed them for diocesan administration, or by the Crown, which was largely dependent upon clerics, from bishops downwards, for running the state (**34, 44**).

Non-residence and pluralism, therefore, remained glaring abuses within the Church, and they helped perpetuate the division of the clergy into a highly paid minority and a clerical proletariat. Among the most highly paid were the bishops. Eleven English sees were worth over £1,000 a year, and a few of them a great deal more – the Bishop of Winchester, for instance, could count on a minimum of £3,500. All bishops were appointed, in effect, by the King, for papal confirmation was a mere formality, and on paper at least they were well qualified. Of thirty-three bishops appointed by Henry VII, fifteen had degrees in law and eight in theology. Cardinal John Morton, whom Henry chose to be Archbishop of Canterbury, was a Doctor of Civil Law and had practised in the ecclesiastical Court of Arches. This sort of education and legal expertise was ideal for administrators, and on the whole the Church was well run. Yet surprisingly enough, since they were not chosen primarily for their spirituality, many bishops took their pastoral duties seriously and worked hard to improve the performance of their diocesan clergy. They were set a good example by Morton, an autocrat by temperament and conservative in outlook, but nevertheless devoted to the interests of the Church and determined to improve its effectiveness within the existing limits (**52, 86**).

Morton was handicapped by the fact that his duties as Lord Chancellor and one of Henry's chief advisers left him insufficient time for ecclesiastical affairs. Much the same was true of his fellow bishops. Richard Fox, for example, began Henry's reign as Bishop of Exeter and was translated from there to Wells, but his official duties as Lord Privy Seal and his unofficial commitments as one of Henry's leading Councillors were so heavy that he never found time to set foot in either cathedral. The consciousness of this neglect of his spiritual duties weighed heavily on him, and towards the end of his life he was glad to abandon the service of the state and devote himself to the see of Winchester, of which he was by then bishop. He also founded Corpus Christi College at Oxford and showed his interest in the new learning of the Renaissance by making provision for lectures in Greek as well as Latin. Another patron of learning was John Fisher, whom Henry appointed Bishop of Rochester in 1504. Fisher was confessor to Henry's mother, Lady Margaret Beaufort, a deeply devout woman who saw the need to strengthen the Christian faith through education. It was at Fisher's suggestion that she instituted the Lady Margaret chairs in divinity at both universities and provided the money for building Christ's College at Cambridge (**52**).

Despite the fact that an increasing proportion of clergy had received a university education there is little indication that they had been affected by the new learning. Many priests possessed books, but they were mainly traditional works of piety, and surprisingly enough they rarely included the Bible. One reason for this may have been the lack of any official translation; those that existed were associated with the Lollards and therefore tainted with heresy. Books of hours, service books and lives of the saints were the usual fare, not only for clergy but also for the literate lay reader, and they were turned out in large numbers by the printing press established at Westminster by John Caxton and taken over, after his death in 1491, by his assistant, Wynkyn de Worde (**25, 34, 44**).

To all appearances the Catholic church in England was firmly established and reasonably popular in the late fifteenth century, but among its most severe critics were the Lollards, who believed that it had become too involved in secular affairs and could only be purified by being stripped of its wealth. The Lollards, whose heretical opinions included a denial of transubstantiation, based their beliefs upon the scriptures, and the Lollard Bible was the only vernacular version circulating in England. Lollardy tended to be strongest in urban areas, such as London, Colchester, Reading, Bristol and Coventry, though it also had adherents in smaller settlements in the Chilterns and Thames Valley region. It appealed most to artisans and small tradesmen, but it had some followers among the urban elites: in Coventry, for example, Richard Cook, who had twice been mayor and represented the town in Parliament during Henry VII's reign, was a Lollard (**34**).

Savage repression during the early years of the fifteenth century had driven Lollardy underground, and for a time it virtually disappeared. Yet this 'disappearance' probably owed more to the breakdown of investigatory machinery in the troubled late-Lancastrian period than to a real decline in numbers. With the restoration of strong rule the ecclesiastical authorities began their investigations once again and soon uncovered evidence of continuing Lollard activity. Over seventy prosecutions for heresy have been recorded for Henry VII's reign. In the great majority of cases the heretics confessed and repented, and were only required to do public penance. However, the handful who remained obdurate were burnt at the stake [**doc. 20**]. Among these was a priest whom Henry himself convinced of his errors while he was actually tied to the stake – though his last-minute recantation did not save him from the flames (**29**).

Henry was entirely orthodox in his religious attitudes, which was just as well, since he needed the support of the Pope for his fledgling dynasty. So conscious was he of the need to maintain good relations with the papal court that in 1492 he asked one of the cardinals resident there to act on his behalf in all matters affecting England. This appointment of a Cardinal Protector was the first to be made by any sovereign and helped ensure a favourable response to the various requests which Henry made (**64**). As a consequence the King had no difficulty in securing papal confirmation of his nominations to the episcopal bench, and he also obtained papal approval for the limited restrictions which he imposed upon the traditional rights of sanctuary and benefit of clergy. Sanctuaries were prescribed areas, usually in or around a religious building, in which criminals could take refuge and be free from arrest as long as they stayed there. Henry was determined that this privilege should not cover traitors, and a judicial decision to this effect was subsequently confirmed by a papal bull. Benefit of clergy was the name given to the practice whereby criminals in holy orders could demonstrate their clerical status by reading through a 'neck verse', whereupon they would be handed over for punishment to the ecclesiastical authorities instead of being dealt with (more harshly) by the common law courts. This privilege had become widely abused, since it extended to those in minor orders, who were clergy only in name, and even to barely-literate laymen. In 1489 therefore, Parliament passed an Act limiting benefit of clergy, except for the first offence, to those who could actually prove that they were in holy orders. There was nothing anti-clerical about either this measure or the restriction of sanctuary. They were both aspects of Henry's campaign to improve the effectiveness of law enforcement.

The Church would have been well advised to abolish minor orders, but it did not do so. Its conservatism, amounting at times to lethargy, prompted a number of individuals to take the lead in pressing for an attack upon abuses. Prominent among these was John Colet, who was famous for his Oxford lectures on the New Testament, and whose associates included William Grocyn, a pioneer of Greek studies in England, Thomas Linacre, a distinguished physician and classicist, and young Thomas More. Erasmus, who came to England for the first time in 1499, was delighted to find such a circle of humanists awaiting him and declared that when he heard Colet speak he felt he was listening to Plato. Colet and his friends were not without their supporters among the hierarchy, principally Richard Fox, John Fisher, and William Warham, the future Archbishop. Henry himself was also sympathetically disposed towards them, as was shown by his appointment of Colet as Dean of St Paul's in 1504 and his later declaration that he intended to provide an English benefice for Erasmus. Yet the hopes of the reformers were not to be fulfilled in Henry's reign, for although the weaknesses of the Church were glaringly apparent there was no obvious way in which to remedy them.

In many respects the Church was the victim of its own success, for it had become a venerable institution, firmly embedded in English society but deeply resistant to change. It inspired loyalty rather than enthusiasm, and this was true of the religious orders as of the clergy as a whole. Yet the monastic vocation had not lost its appeal, and by the time Henry died there were probably more men and women in religious orders than at any time since the Black Death. And although standards in general had slipped, there were shining exceptions, principal among them the Carthusians. The friars, who had in many instances retained their commitment to holy poverty, were also popular, judged by the number of bequests left to them, and Henry showed a great liking for the Franciscans. It may be that he favoured the Observants, who had returned to the original rule of St Francis, rather than the Conventuals, who were less austere, but in practice he gave his patronage more or less equally to both branches (**102**).

The overall picture of the *Ecclesia Anglicana* in Henry VII's reign is that of an institution which, despite its obvious flaws, commanded the voluntary allegiance of the great majority of the English people, from the King downwards. Evidence of this survives to the present day, for Henry's munificence in adding to Westminster Abbey the resplendent Perpendicular chapel which bears his name was matched by corporations, gilds, and ordinary men and women throughout the land. The late fifteenth and early sixteenth centuries saw the rebuilding and beautifying of many parish churches, and the fact that people were prepared to spend their money in this way must surely be taken as an indication that the Church, for all its faults, was a valued and integral part of English society.

9. The Economy

Enclosures

The economy of England in Henry VII's reign was based upon agriculture, most of which was for subsistence, and its health fluctuated with the quality of the harvests. The early 1480s had been bad years, but in 1485, the year of Henry's accession, the harvest was good, and this upturn was maintained right through the 1490s. Good harvests undoubtedly promoted social stability and helped Henry in the task of establishing his new dynasty. But his luck ran out in the closing decade of his reign, and there were four bad harvests in a row between 1500 and 1503 – a period of dearth which helps to explain the concern for public order shown in the parliament of 1504 (**90**).

Apart from food the most important single commodity was wool, which formed the basis of England's major industry and accounted, indirectly, for some ninety per cent of English exports. The demand for wool had a marked effect upon the pattern of English farming, since many farmers found it more profitable to turn their estates over to sheep than to continue cultivating them in the traditional manner. This affected the rural community in three main ways, through enclosure, engrossing and depopulation – an unholy trinity which came to be the bugbear of Tudor governments.

Enclosure meant, strictly speaking, the fencing-off of a man's property and the extinguishing of common rights over it, so that it could be cultivated without reference to the community. The advantage of enclosure was that it enabled the progressive farmer to develop his own techniques, without being held back by the incompetence, conservatism or laziness of his neighbours. In particular it made it possible for him to practise selective breeding of animals, especially sheep, in order to improve the quality of his stock. The main objection to enclosure was that it often led to the eviction of families which had settled in the affected area without ever establishing a legal tenure. Freeholders could claim a share of the land to be enclosed; copyholders also had a right to compensation, which could be enforced in Chancery and the prerogative courts if the common law courts (which were, in fact, beginning to take cognisance of copyholds during Henry's reign) refused to act. But tenants-at-will, cottagers and squatters were unprotected at law, and if they were evicted had no resources and nowhere to go.

Enclosure – using this term, as contemporaries did, to include engrossing – was a frequent cause of riots in Henry's reign. At Coventry, for instance, in 1496, the rich burgesses of the town council decided to enclose the Lammas fields on which many of the inhabitants grazed their sheep and cattle. The opposition to this move was led by one of the townsmen, who distributed propaganda verses such as those which started

> The city is bond that should be free.
> The right is holden from the commonalty.
> Our commons, that at Lammas open should be cast,
> They be closed in and hedged full fast (**16**, vol. 3, p. 13).

As far as the destruction of villages was concerned, most of the damage had been done before Henry VII came to the throne, but his government was sufficiently alarmed to pass the first legislation against the practice. An Act of 1489 was specifically directed to the Isle of Wight, which because of conversion of arable to pasture and engrossing, was said to be 'desolate and not inhabited, but occupied with beasts and cattle'. The same year also saw a general Act which, while it made no specific reference to enclosure, recited how 'great inconveniences daily doth increase by desolation and pulling-down and wilful waste of houses and towns within this . . . realm, and laying to pasture lands which customably have been used in tilth', and complained that 'where in some towns two hundred persons were occupied and lived by their lawful labours, now be there occupied two or three herdsmen'. However, the only remedy provided by the Act was an order that all towns and houses should in future be maintained and not allowed to decay – a pious hope but not very effective in halting the economic forces that were transforming the countryside.

Although Henry VII's government, like that of his successors, was formally opposed to depopulating enclosures, some of the chief offenders were themselves in royal service. At Wormleighton, for example, on the borders of Warwickshire and Northamptonshire, William Cope, Cofferer of the Household, evicted the inhabitants of fifteen tenements in October 1498, enclosed two hundred and forty acres of arable with hedges and ditches, and turned the newly created field over to sheep. Sixty persons lost their dwellings as a result of this particular operation and were forced to depart 'tearfully' (**22, 23**). Another of Henry's officers who was accused of depopulating enclosures was Edward Belknap. Yet it should be added that in both these cases, and perhaps in many others in the midland region of England, the villages which were destroyed had long been declining and had perhaps reached the stage where they were no longer economically viable. Enclosures, then, did not always, or necessarily, imply an abrupt change of course forced upon a community by the greed of unprincipled landlords – many of whom, in practice, would have been only too happy to see the villages which they owned prosper and develop. Enclosures could also be the virtually inevitable conclusion to a process of decay that had been taking place over many decades (**71, 77**).

Wool and cloth

The obverse of this gloomy picture is the prosperity of the trade in wool and woollen cloth, and of the towns and villages – mainly in the Midlands and East Anglia – which thrived on it. The clothier was a familiar figure in Henry VII's England, riding round the country buying wool, arranging for its collection and distribution to centres where it could either be packed for export or else woven into cloth. Export of raw wool had been declining because of the heavy taxation imposed on it, as well as the growing demand of the native cloth industry. This decline continued throughout Henry's reign, and by 1509 wool exports were some thirty per cent lower than they had been in 1485. This affected the Merchants of the Staple, who had a monopoly of the export of raw wool to Calais, the staple town, and were financially responsible for the maintenance of the garrison there. But while the trade in raw wool was shrinking, the export of cloth was flourishing, and sixty per cent more cloth was being sent abroad by the end of Henry's reign than had been exported in the early years.

The leading part in the export of cloth was taken by the Merchant Adventurers of London, who dominated the trade with Antwerp. The trouble with the London Adventurers was that they wanted to establish a monopoly of all cloth exports, and this was resented by the merchants of the 'outports' – particularly towns like Bristol and Boston. The London company took the first step towards establishing a monopoly in 1496, when it declared that anyone trading in cloth should pay it a fee of £20. This was a prohibitively high sum, designed to limit the numbers of people involved so that the profit level would be high. Such high-handed action brought the company up against parliament, where the Londoners were in a minority, and an Act of the following year condemned the Adventurers' demand as springing from 'their uncharitable and inordinate covetousness' and commanded them to reduce their fee by two-thirds.

While Henry was willing to restrain the Merchant Adventurers at home for fear that they would constrict trade instead of expanding it, he gave them full support abroad. In 1505 a royal charter authorised the company to inspect cloth and maintain standards of quality, and also to settle disputes and take whatever other measures it thought necessary for the efficient functioning of the trade. The Adventurers' entrance fee was now fixed at £5 – the implication being that they could have a virtual monopoly of cloth exports on condition that they did not attempt to confine membership to an oligarchy of rich men.

The main outlet for the sale of English cloth was Antwerp, which was rapidly becoming the commercial capital of Europe. Yet while English merchants valued Antwerp for its convenience, they were not dependent on it. Cloth was so necessary a commodity that buyers would follow wherever the market moved. The factories of Flanders, on the other hand, which specialised in refining the coarse English cloth and turning it into a variety of fabrics, were firmly fixed, and this gave Henry a weapon he did not hesitate to use. In 1493, when the ruler of the Netherlands was giving support to the pretender Perkin Warbeck, Henry ordered the Adventurers to move to Calais, and his embargo on trade with the Netherlands remained in force until 1496. The Netherlands retaliated with a counterembargo on English goods, and although trade between the two countries did not dry up completely it was irregular and restricted. A return to sanity was signalled by the signing of the *Magnus Intercursus* in 1496. Under the terms of this agreement English merchants were free to sell their goods wholesale anywhere in the Duke of Burgundy's dominions except Flanders itself, and were guaranteed swift and fair justice, a regular machinery for the settlement of disputes, and immunity from new tolls or duties.

The *Magnus Intercursus* did not, in practice, put an end to disputes between the Merchant Adventurers and the government of the Netherlands. However, Henry found his bargaining power unexpectedly strengthened when gales drove Philip, Duke of Burgundy, into an English port in 1506. Philip now became the guest of Henry, who persuaded him to agree to a commercial treaty giving English merchants unprecedented privileges. The name given by Bacon to this agreement – *Malus Intercursus* – is accurate enough, since instead of being based, like the *Magnus Intercursus*, on principles that would provide the maximum benefit for both sides, it was extorted by Henry out of Philip's weakness and was likely to cause so much offence in the Netherlands that the English merchants would gain little by it. In fact the treaty, which was followed shortly afterwards by Philip's death, never became fully operative, and in 1507 another agreement confirmed the *Magnus Intercursus* as the basis for trading relations between the two countries (**63**).

The expansion of overseas trade

While Henry encouraged the vital trade between England and the Netherlands, he also used diplomacy to increase the share of English merchants in other markets. There was quite a flourishing trade in existence between France and England, based on wine from Gascony and woad from Toulouse, and the Navigation Acts of 1485 and 1489 (see below, p. 65) were designed to give English ships a commanding position in this. In 1486 Henry signed a commercial agreement with France, removing the restrictions that had hampered Anglo-French trade since the days of Edward IV. But the quarrel over Brittany, with which Henry had also made a treaty of commerce, led the French to reimpose the restrictions on English merchants. Not until 1495 were they entirely swept away – part of the price that France had to pay for English neutrality during the Italian wars – and in 1497 a new treaty of commerce confirmed the privileges of the English merchants trading with the King of France's dominions.

Further south Henry renewed, in 1489, the treaty of friendship with Portugal concluded over a hundred years earlier. He also took steps to increase the part played by English merchants in trade with Spain. By the commercial clauses of the treaty of Medina del Campo, signed in 1489, it was agreed that English and Spanish merchants should have reciprocal rights in each others' countries, and that duties should be fixed at low rates. English merchants gradually began to increase their share of Anglo-Spanish trade, particularly after the Navigation Acts. These were so effective that Spain retaliated with Navigation Acts of her own, forbidding the export of goods from Spain in foreign ships when native ones were available. With trade confined in one direction to Spanish ships, and in the other to English ones, the volume decreased, and although English merchants were more firmly entrenched in Anglo-Spanish trade at the end of Henry's reign than they had been at the beginning, the policies of each government served only to check the expansion of commerce.

Since the middle of the fifteenth century English merchants had been pushing into the Mediterranean region, buying wines from Crete and currants from the Levant. This brought them up against Venice, which had established a virtual monopoly over trade in the eastern Mediterranean and resented any threat to the commercial wealth upon which her greatness depended. The Venetians therefore imposed a heavy duty upon wines taken from their possessions in foreign ships, hoping that by doing so they would preserve the privileged position of their own galleys, which made annual sailings to Europe and used Southampton as their port of call in England. Henry could not challenge Venice direct, but he could intrigue with her rivals, chief among whom was Florence. In 1490, therefore, Henry concluded a trade treaty with Florence and agreed that the Florentine port of Pisa should be a staple for English wool, which should be carried there in English ships. Two years later he took more specific retaliatory action against Venice by imposing a heavy duty on wines brought to England in Venetian ships. This tariff war might have continued indefinitely but for the intervention of France and Spain in Italy, which left the Venetians so preoccupied at home that they were unable to give much attention to a peripheral commercial squabble. By the time Henry died, therefore, English merchants had built up a regular trade to Pisa and the Levant (**56**).

The challenge to Venice was one of the reasons which led Henry to patronise those explorers who believed that a route to the east, with its fabulous silks and spices, could be found by sailing west, thereby outflanking the Venetian domination of the established trade routes. Henry narrowly missed becoming the patron of Columbus, but in 1496 he issued letters patent to John Cabot authorising him 'to sail to all parts, regions and coasts of the eastern, western and northern sea'. When Cabot returned from his first voyage of 1497, during which he discovered Newfoundland, Henry gave him audience, listened attentively to his account of his adventures, and encouraged him to set out again the following year [**doc. 21**]. Cabot never returned from his second voyage, but

Henry extended royal patronage to his son, Sebastian, authorising him to settle any territories which were not already occupied by Christian states. In 1506 the Bristol company of 'Adventurers in the New Found Lands' was formed, and this backed Sebastian Cabot's next voyage, in which he probably explored Hudson Bay and the North American coast. By the time he returned home, however, Henry VII was dead, and with him any hope that England might join Spain and Portugal among the pioneers of exploration and settlement in the New World.

In his dealings with France, Spain and Venice Henry was reasonably successful. Further north, however, he had a much more stubborn competitor to reckon with in the shape of the German cities of the Hanseatic League, whose headquarters was at Lübeck. The Hansards dominated the trade of northern Europe and enjoyed a highly favoured position even within England, since Edward IV had granted them exceptional privileges in return for their support. At London (where they were based in the Steelyard) and at Southampton and Boston they had established depots which were virtually autonomous states. They could live where they pleased; they could sell certain goods retail; they were partially exempt from taxation; and they paid lower duties on goods they exported than those which were paid by English merchants.

The privileged status of the Hansards provoked deep resentment, but although Henry shared this he had to move carefully. For one thing the Hanse could cause him a lot of trouble if it chose to support pretenders to the English throne; and, for another, England was dependent on the Hanse for a considerable part of her foreign trade and he could not afford to disrupt this. In March 1486, therefore, Henry confirmed the privileges of the Hanse in England, but he began to outflank them in other ways. An Act of parliament of the next year ordered that no aliens, including Hansards, should export unfinished cloth, and two years later they were forbidden to take money or bullion out of the country. Henry tacitly encouraged the protest of his subjects against the privileges of the Hanse. When in 1493 a London mob attacked the Steelyard Henry paid little compensation, and later demanded £20,000 as security for the Hansards' promise that they would not trade with the Netherlands while an embargo was in force. The King confiscated this sum in 1508, because, he claimed, the Hansards had broken their promise. Henry also claimed that the Hansards' privilege of importing goods at a low rate of duty applied only to items originating from Hansa towns and territories, and not to those which the merchants gathered from all over Europe. When the Hanse protested, Henry refused to listen (**56, 63**).

Henry's aim was to give English merchants direct access to the valuable Baltic market, where their woollen cloth would be welcome, and from which they could obtain essential naval stores and corn. Just as he used Florence to outflank Venice in the Mediterranean, so he used the Hanse's rivals to challenge the monopoly of the League in northern waters. In 1489 he made an alliance with Denmark, extended in 1490, which gave English merchants freedom to trade in Denmark and Norway and the right to fish in Icelandic waters. The struggle with the League continued throughout Henry's reign, except for a brief period in 1504 when Henry, in a sudden *volte-face*, confirmed the privileges of the Hanse as they had been in Edward IV's day. This otherwise inexplicable action seems to have resulted from a moment of panic when the Earl of Suffolk – the latest of the pretenders with whom Henry had to contend – fled to north Germany and looked to the League to help him. Once the immediate danger had passed, the King returned to his old policy of whittling down the League's privileges. Yet his success was limited, for the League was too rich and too powerful for Henry alone to overthrow, and English shipping had not developed to the point where it could fill any vacuum that might be created by Henry's diplomacy.

The encouragement of English shipping

The weakness of English shipping was part of a vicious circle. While Hansard ships were available there was little incentive for the building of English ones, yet the lack of English ships meant that there was no possibility of mounting an effective challenge to the Hanse. Those members of the Commons with commercial interests were well aware of the need to remedy this situation, and it was probably pressure from them rather than any initiative on Henry's part that led to the passing of the Navigation Acts of 1485 and 1489. The first Act, calling to mind 'the great [di]minishing and decay that hath been now of late time of the navy within this realm of England, and idleness of the mariners within the same, by the which this noble realm within short process of time, without reformation be had therein, shall not be of ability and power to defend itself', ordered that in future wines from Guienne and Gascony should be imported only in English ships with a predominantly English crew [**doc. 22**]. The 1489 Act added a general provision that English merchants (the prohibition did not apply to aliens) should not import any goods in foreign ships when English ones were available. The outcry from the Hansards, as well as the issuing of similar legislation by Spain, suggests that this early exercise in mercantilism was comparatively successful.

The connexion between merchant shipping and naval defence was very close, since merchant vessels became warships in times of crisis. Edward IV had reconstructed a royal navy, and Richard III took a similar interest in naval matters, maintaining a fleet of some ten ships. Henry VII was not so committed and by the end of his reign there were only five 'King's Ships' – though they included the 600-tonne *Regent*, which carried 225 guns, and the *Sovereign*, with 141. Henry did, however, improve the operational range and effectiveness of his small navy by constructing its first dry dock, at Portsmouth, and he also developed the Thames ports and established arsenals at Greenwich and Woolwich (**100**).

Henry, like Edward IV, was personally involved in trade. He imported alum, which was essential for the manufacture of soap, and in 1505–06 made £15,000 from the sale of this commodity. He hired out royal ships, and he also made interest-free loans to English and foreign merchants on condition that their trade benefited the Customs by an agreed amount [**doc. 3**]. Customs gave Henry an obvious financial interest in the state of trade. He appointed a commission to see whether he was being cheated by smuggling on the south coast and in the west country, but in fact smuggling seems to have been relatively small-scale (**98**). He also introduced a new Book of Rates in 1507, although this probably applied only to London. The yield from Customs would presumably have increased without any royal encouragement, as conditions became more stable and trade expanded, but the rise of over 20 per cent, from some £33,000 in 1485 to more than £40,000 by 1509, was a considerable achievement.

It is impossible to say to what extent Henry's policies were of direct benefit to English trade. In the north his success was limited, in southern Europe it was greater. But these were minor outlets compared with the vital link between England and the Netherlands, and the volume of trade here was determined rather by reciprocal needs than conscious acts of policy. Even the proportion of this trade in the hands of alien merchants remained much the same throughout the reign. English merchants had the greater part, some 53 per cent; the Hanse accounted for a further 24 per cent, and other aliens for the rest. The only conclusion that can be drawn from these figures is that without Henry's encouragement of English commerce the share of English merchants in trade from this country might have declined. The long-term effect of his policy was perhaps more important, in that he sketched out the lines – into the Baltic, the Mediterranean, and across the Atlantic – along which English commerce was eventually to develop.

10 Ireland, Scotland and Foreign Affairs

The states of Western Europe

Western Europe during the period of Henry VII's reign was dominated by two great states, France and Spain, and, to a lesser extent, by the Holy Roman Emperor.

The general tenor of French policy was in the direction of an extension of the frontiers of France to her 'natural' boundaries, although this was never consistently or consciously pursued and gained its greatest triumphs as much by accident as by design. Louis XI had been particularly successful, and by the time he died, in 1483, had nearly doubled the amount of territory held by the French crown. He left as his heir the thirteen-year-old Charles VIII.

Spain had been united only in 1479, ten years after the marriage of Ferdinand, King of Aragon, to Isabella, Queen of Castile. The southern part of the peninsula was still, however, occupied by the Moors, and Ferdinand and Isabella made it their lives' work to drive them out. In this they were successful, and in 1492, just before Columbus set off on a journey that would give them a whole new world to rule, they completed the conquest of the last Moorish kingdom, Granada.

Ten years before Henry VIII came to the throne of England it looked as though Burgundy would develop into one of the major states of Europe, but in 1477 its great duke, Charles the Bold, died, and his territories were divided. The Netherlands went to his daughter Mary, who in 1477 married the young Archduke Maximilian of Austria. In 1493, following the death of his father, the Emperor Frederick III, Maximilian was elected to the Imperial throne, and since by this time Mary was dead, the government of the Netherlands devolved upon their son Philip, Duke of Burgundy.

Ireland

In the opening years of his reign Henry had to face a number of challenges from the Yorkists, who had not been reconciled by his marriage, in January 1486, to Edward IV's daughter, Elizabeth of York. The first of these, Lord Lovell's rising, fortunately collapsed before it came to anything, but it was followed by a more serious conspiracy which had its roots in Ireland.

Henry was nominally Lord of Ireland, but in practice English rule was confined to the 'Pale', a strip of coast some twenty miles wide and fifty miles long, stretching from just south of Dublin northwards to Dundalk. Beyond the Pale the real rulers of Ireland were the descendants of the Anglo-Norman barons, and the major motivating force in politics was the family quarrel between the Butlers and the Geraldines. The head of the Geraldines was the Earl of Kildare, whom Henry retained as Lord Deputy despite the fact that he had Yorkist sympathies. Kildare's loyalty was tested, and found wanting, in 1486 when the Yorkists brought forward Lambert Simnel, the twelve-year-old son of an organ-builder, and declared that he was in fact Edward IV's nephew, the Earl of Warwick, and therefore the rightful ruler of England and Ireland. Simnel was just a figurehead, of course, but the conspirators included Richard III's nephew, the Earl of Lincoln, whom Richard had nominated as his successor. The Yorkist lords 'persuaded' Kildare to recognise Simnel as King, and on Whitsunday 1486 the boy was solemnly crowned in Dublin cathedral as Edward VI. Troops had already been raised, including two thousand German mercenaries provided by Edward IV's sister Margaret, the widow of Charles the Bold of Burgundy. In June 1487 the rebel force landed in Lancashire and swiftly advanced towards Newark. Henry caught them just outside the town, near the village of Stoke, and after three hours of savage fighting routed them. Lincoln was killed. Simnel was captured and began a new, and less glamorous, career as a turnspit in the royal kitchens.

Although Stoke was a victory for Henry, it showed up the weakness of his position. The fact that so transparent a pretender had been acclaimed in one of his dominions and had only been defeated after a bloody battle in which half of the King's forces – through mischance, or, more likely, lack of commitment on the part of their commanders – had never become engaged, was evidence of the slender nature of Henry's hold on the throne and of the potential strength of his enemies. The attainders that followed, when parliament assembled, were evidence that Henry recognised this and was determined to strengthen his grip.

Brittany

No sooner had Henry overcome a threat to his position at home than he was confronted with one from abroad, for in 1487 Charles VIII of France invaded the independent Duchy of Brittany, with the obvious intention of incorporating it into his kingdom. Brittany acted as a buffer between England and France, and Henry was determined to maintain its independence, but although he despatched a volunteer force to aid the duke, he could not prevent the defeat of the Breton army in July 1488. This was shortly followed by the death of the duke, leaving his twelve-year-old daughter, Anne, as reigning duchess.

It now seemed inevitable that Henry would have to intervene, and in January 1489 he summoned a parliament which voted £100,000 for raising an army. He also looked for allies, and found one in Ferdinand of Spain, who had his own reasons for joining in an attack upon France, but refused to do so unless Henry promised not to make a separate peace. The acceptance of this condition meant tying English strategy to the fulfilment of Spanish ambitions, but Henry saw no alternative and he therefore gave the required assurance in the treaty of Medina del Campo of 1489. He was persuaded to do so not simply by the fact that he needed Spanish support but also by the clauses in the treaty whereby Ferdinand and Isabella bound themselves not to allow any Yorkist pretenders to take refuge on Spanish soil, and to promote a marriage between their daughter, Catherine, and Henry's eldest son, Prince Arthur. Such an alliance would mark acceptance of the Tudor dynasty by one of the greatest powers in Europe, and would increase Henry's prestige at home as well as abroad. Henry's pride in this achievement may be indicated by the fact that he chose this moment to issue a new coin, the golden sovereign, on which he was shown wearing not the traditional open crown of Kings of England but an imperial crown, closed over the head with hoops. It was a clear statement of Henry's belief that he was now the equal of any ruler in Christendom (**28**).

The treaty of Medina del Campo was concluded in March 1489, but in the previous month the treaty of Redon, between England and Brittany, had bound the Duchess Anne to pay the cost of an English expeditionary force of 6,000 men, and to hand over Morlaix and Concarneau as sureties. Before the end of April English troops were in action in Brittany, but their success was slight, and although they were joined by a small Spanish force in 1490 this was quickly withdrawn for service against the Moors. The steady advance of the French into Brittany continued, and in December 1491 Anne bowed to the inevitable and agreed to marry Charles VIII. The days of Breton independence were now clearly numbered.

Henry was left committed to war for a purpose which could no longer be achieved. Withdrawal at this stage would have been as ignominious as defeat, yet the only alternative was to become even more involved. It seems unlikely that Henry really contemplated a major war against France, but he acted as though he did, no doubt aware that he would get better terms from France by displaying his power than by tamely accepting the *fait accompli*. He had before him the example of Edward IV, who had conducted a magnificent foray into France (for which parliament had provided the money) and had been rewarded by the treaty of Picquigny, which guaranteed him a French pension for the rest of his life. Henry accordingly announced his intention to enforce his claim to the French throne, sent out his agents to collect a Benevolence in the summer of 1491, and summoned parliament in the winter to make a more formal and legitimate grant. In October 1492 he crossed the Channel at the head of an army of 26,000 men, having waited until near the end of the campaigning season so that if he were forced to fight it could not be for long. His strategy was successful. Charles VIII had ambitions of his own in Italy and did not want to waste time, men and money on the relief of Boulogne, now under siege by Henry. A month after the English landing, therefore, the treaty of Etaples put an end to the state of war between the two countries. Henry did not abandon his claim to the French throne, but he agreed to withdraw his army in return for a promise that no French aid would be forthcoming for Yorkist pretenders and that he, like Edward IV before him, should become the recipient of a French pension. Henry could hardly claim a glorious victory, for he had entered the war in order to preserve Brittany, and Brittany had been lost. But he had gained a Spanish alliance and made a significant addition to his annual income. These were items to be set down on the credit side of the balance sheet (**63**).

Perkin Warbeck

The provision about Yorkist pretenders in the treaty of Etaples was no mere form of words, for in October 1491 another had already appeared on the scene. This was Perkin Warbeck, the son of a

Tournai Customs officer who became apprenticed to a merchant and went with him to Cork, in Ireland. There he was spotted by a group of Yorkist conspirators, who thought he might serve their turn. They eventually persuaded him to impersonate Richard, Duke of York – one of the two children of Edward IV who had been murdered in the Tower. The King of France, then at war with England, made Warbeck welcome at his court until the conclusion of peace at Etaples. The pretender then made his way to the Netherlands, where Margaret of Burgundy – whose devotion to her family cause never faltered – acknowledged him as her nephew and promised him support.

Henry could not do anything effective to dislodge Warbeck from the Netherlands – although he imposed an embargo on Anglo-Flemish trade in 1493 – but he acted firmly against possible fomentors of rebellion nearer home. Lord Fitzwalter and other Yorkist conspirators were arrested and executed in 1491, and they were followed to the block in the next year by Sir William Stanley. As for Ireland, Henry had decided on a radical change of course. Instead of continuing to rule through the established Irish families he appointed his baby son, Prince Henry, as Lieutenant of Ireland and made Sir Edward Poynings his deputy. Poynings was given an army with which to enforce the King's will and was accompanied by a number of English officials, including financial experts. Henry was obviously planning to bring Ireland under the same sort of household administration that marked his rule in England, and thereby ensure that the institutions of Irish government should never again be placed at the disposal of Yorkist pretenders (**26**).

Poynings was successful in restoring order, and he then summoned the Irish parliament to meet at Drogheda in December 1494. Business began with the attainder of Kildare, who was sent prisoner to England, and it continued with the passing of numerous Acts designed to bring Irish administration under the control of the English Crown. The culminating measure of this parliament was the statute which became known as 'Poynings' Law' and which laid down that in future no Irish parliament should meet or pass any legislation without first obtaining the approval of the English government.

Among the financial experts whom Henry sent over to Ireland was Henry Wyatt. Henry seems to have hoped that Wyatt would find a way to make Ireland pay for the costs of governing it, but in this he was disappointed. Wyatt's figures made it plain that Ireland could not even pay for the upkeep of its permanent garrison, let alone expeditionary forces like that of Poynings. If Henry was to transform his nominal overlordship into an actual one he would have to spend a great deal of money, and this he was not prepared to do. However, he left Poynings in Ireland for the time being, since there was still a threat that Warbeck might reappear. This threat materialised in 1495, when the pretender landed in Ireland, was joined by the Earl of Desmond and other malcontents, and besieged Waterford, the second most important town in the country. But Waterford, with help from Poynings, defied the besiegers, and Warbeck eventually abandoned the attempt and sailed away to Scotland. By the end of 1495 Ireland had been pacified, and Poynings returned to England. Henry, who needed money and men for operations against Scotland, now disentangled himself from his Irish involvement and returned to the practice of ruling through the Irish magnates. He had been impressed by Kildare, and when it was pointed out to him that 'All England cannot rule yonder gentleman', he replied 'No? Then he is mete to rule all Ireland'. Kildare was therefore reinstated as Deputy, having abandoned his Yorkist inclinations, and Ireland ceased to be a major problem for Henry (**78**).

The storm-centre shifted with Warbeck to Scotland. When Henry had been an exile relations between him and James III of Scotland had been good, but in 1488 James was overthrown and killed in a rebellion, and his son ascended the throne as James IV. Henry quickly concluded a three-year truce with the new king, which was later extended into a seven-year one. But these paper agreements were not worth much. In fact James IV was only waiting for a good opportunity to renew the struggle against England. The opportunity seemed at hand in 1495, when Warbeck landed in Scotland after his abortive attempt to raise Ireland. James entertained Warbeck regally and gave him his cousin, Lady Catherine Gordon, as wife. He also set on foot preparations for an invasion of England. But when the attempt was made at last, in September 1496, it was a fiasco. Warbeck called on the northern counties of England to rise against the 'usurper' Henry, but there was no response, and as soon as the Scots troops heard that English forces were moving against them they fled back across the border (**63**).

Although the invasion had come to nothing, Henry could not ignore the challenge thrown down by James IV. In October 1496 he summoned a *magnum concilium* which made a grant of money for the prosecution of war against the Scots, and this was confirmed by the parliament of January 1497 which, not content with voting two fifteenths and tenths, added a subsidy 'for their necessary defence against the cruel malice of the Scots'. Henry went ahead with preparations for his campaign, but in June 1497, while his armies were mustering in the north, the inhabitants of Cornwall rose in revolt against the levying of taxes for a war which meant nothing to them. Although the rebels were poorly led they surged through the western counties and by the middle of June were on the outskirts of London. Henry summoned Lord Daubeny, whom he had sent to command the northern armies, to return south at full speed, bringing his troops with him and leaving the defence of the border to local levies. No sooner had Daubeny arrived than he encircled the Cornish rebels, who were encamped on Blackheath, ready to strike at London. The Cornishmen fought bravely but the odds were against them and they were heavily defeated. Their ringleaders were captured and executed. The rank and file were left to stream back to Cornwall the way they had come.

The Cornish rebellion showed Henry that he could not afford to become entangled in Scotland any more than in Ireland. There was now a good chance of a negotiated settlement, for James IV, who had taken advantage of the Cornish rising to invade England once again, had been chased back over the border by the Earl of Surrey. In September 1497, therefore, the truce of Ayton was signed, putting an end to the war between the two countries. Five years later, in 1502, this was extended into a treaty of peace and alliance, to be cemented by a marriage between James and Henry's daughter, Margaret. The marriage took place the following year, and the fragile peace established at Ayton lasted for the rest of Henry's reign (**63**).

Warbeck had left Scotland before the truce was agreed upon. In July 1497 he landed at Cork, hoping to find Ireland as welcoming as before to Yorkist claimants. But Kildare now held true to Henry Tudor, and the citizens of Waterford showed their attitude by sending ships to catch Warbeck. By this time, however, the pretender had already left for Cornwall, where he hoped to be received in a more friendly fashion. Although Henry had treated the west country with remarkable leniency after the Cornish rising, discontent still smouldered there, and several thousand men flocked to join Warbeck. But the King had received warning from Ireland about the pretender's plans, and Daubeny was already on his way westward with a royal army. In the event there was no need for a pitched battle. Warbeck was beaten off by the citizens of Exeter as he attempted to take the town by storm, and when he heard that Daubeny's forces were closing in on him he abandoned his troops and fled to sanctuary at Beaulieu Abbey near Southampton. There he surrendered, and in early October appeared before Henry at Taunton, where he made a full confession of his imposture. Warbeck could hardly have expected merciful treatment at Henry's hands, since he had caused the King more anxiety and expense than any other single person. Yet Henry kept him under mild captivity, and only transferred him to the Tower after Warbeck had attempted to escape. Warbeck, the false duke, and Warwick, the real earl, were now prisoners together, and soon the plotting began again. This time Henry showed no mercy. In November 1499 Warbeck and Warwick were both executed for treason. Warbeck was hanged at Tyburn. Warwick, as befitted a true member of the blood royal, was beheaded on Tower Hill.

The closing years of the reign

By the time Warbeck and Warwick met their ends, Henry was firmly established on the throne, and there was no obvious threat to him from abroad, since France and Spain were locked in combat for possession of the rich cities of Italy. Spain was anxious to enrol England on her side against France in the so-called Holy League – the sanctity of which came from the fact that the Pope was also a partner – and she used her influence to persuade the Emperor Maximilian to stop supporting Yorkist pretenders and to consent to the restoration of full trade between England and the Netherlands. This was confirmed in the *Magnus Intercursus*, signed in February 1496, and a few months later Henry formally joined the Holy League. Unlike the other members, however, he did not commit himself to take aggressive action against France, with which he retained friendly relations, which were renewed after the death of Charles VIII in 1498 and the accession of Louis XII. Ferdinand and Isabella of Spain also professed their friendship for the new King of France, but they had few illusions about his intentions to renew the struggle for Italy, and they remained committed to the building up of an anti-French coalition. To encourage Henry to join this they allowed the marriage provisions of the treaty of Medina del Campo to be put into effect. In August 1497 the formal betrothal of Prince Arthur and Catherine of Aragon was announced, but the princess herself did not arrive in England until the winter of 1501. In November of that year the marriage at last took place and the future of the Tudor dynasty seemed assured (**63**).

This assurance was short-lived, however, and the problem of the succession became once again acute in the closing years of the reign. In April 1502 Prince Arthur died, to be followed, a year later, by his mother, Queen Elizabeth. The future of the dynasty now depended upon the life of the King's second son, Prince Henry, who was unmarried, and as if to emphasise the fragility of the Tudor hold upon the throne, Yorkist plotting started up again. This time it centred round Edmund de la Pole, Earl of Suffolk, the brother of the Earl of Lincoln who had been nominated by Richard III as his successor but had been killed at Stoke in 1487. Henry was alerted and took precautions, but could not stop Suffolk from fleeing abroad. However, all those suspected of being involved in his conspiracy were arrested, many of them were attainted and executed, and in January 1504 parliament passed Acts forbidding unauthorised assemblies and providing heavy penalties for those who let prisoners escape. The atmosphere of these years is recaptured by an informer's report to the council of a discussion held among 'many great personages' at Calais. They were considering what would happen after Henry's death, and the informant recalled how 'some of them spake of my lord of Buckingham, saying that he was a noble man and would be a royal ruler. Other there were that spake in like wise of your traitor, Edmund de la Pole; but none of them spake of my lord prince' (**8** pp. 5–6).

The need to secure his dynasty drove Henry to consider not only the marriage of his surviving son but also the possibilities of a second marriage for himself. So far as Prince Henry was concerned Ferdinand and Isabella were anxious that he should marry the widowed Catherine, and this was agreed, in principle, in 1503. The King's own matrimonial projects varied with the rapidly changing situation in Europe, but by 1505 he was drawing closer to Burgundy and discussing the possibility of marrying Margaret of Savoy, the sister of Philip, Duke of Burgundy. In January 1506 Philip, who was *en route* by sea to Castile, was driven by violent storms into Weymouth. Henry invited him to Windsor and took advantage of this impromptu encounter to draw the bonds between England and the Netherlands even closer. Philip agreed to hand over the Earl of Suffolk and to do what he could to bring about the marriage between Henry and Margaret of Savoy. He also agreed to the *Malus Intercursus*, with its highly favourable terms for English merchants trading with the Netherlands (see above, p. 62).

The death of Philip in September 1506 brought this diplomatic card-house to the ground, but Henry's main aim was still the preservation of the Netherlands against possible French occupation, and he therefore concentrated his efforts on maintaining the alliance. He achieved this in December 1507, when the Emperor Maximilian agreed that his grandson and ward, Charles – the son of Philip of Burgundy, and therefore the nominal ruler of the Netherlands – should in due course marry Henry's daughter Mary. Henry meanwhile continued to press his own suit with Margaret of Savoy, but her determination was a match for his own, and she made it clear that even the prospect of a crown did not tempt her (**63**).

Henry's foreign policy was not the product of a master-plan carefully worked out and consistently applied. It was the reaction to constantly changing circumstances created by the rivalries of the great powers of Europe, among which England was hardly to be numbered. He did, of course, have certain principles in mind: the protection of his dynasty against Yorkist pretenders; the safeguarding of the independence of the Netherlands; and the promotion of English trade. But he never tried to act as the arbiter of Europe, nor as the peacemaker, since he could not hope to hold back France and Spain, and in any case their involvement in Italy kept them from intrigues against England. He took advantage of favourable circumstances to tie his family into the ruling houses of Europe, but he could not afford to indulge in large-scale military ventures as his fellow sovereigns did, and he made his overriding aim the accumulation and conservation of wealth rather than its dissipation. His foreign policy, then, was lacking in glamour, and its successes owed as much to luck as to judgement. Nevertheless there was good reason for Henry to be proud of how it had all turned out, and there was justice in the claim which he made to the city of London in December 1507, that 'This our realm is now environed and, in manner, closed in every side with such mighty princes our good sons, friends, confederates and allies, that by the help of our Lord the same is and shall be perpetually established in rest and peace and wealthy condition'.

Part Three: Assessment

11 Conclusion

When John Richard Green published his *Short History of the English People* in 1874, he entitled the chapter which dealt with events from 1471 to 1509 'The New Monarchy'. He made his reasons for so doing perfectly clear. English constitutional development, as he saw it, had been progressing very nicely under the Lancastrians, with the liberties of the subject protected and strengthened by an active parliament, a time-honoured system of law with which no mere ruler could interfere, and the beginnings of commercial expansion. All this was brought to an end by the Wars of the Roses, for these did 'far more than ruin one royal house or set up another on the throne. If they did not utterly destroy English freedom, they arrested its progress for more than a hundred years'. The people of England had been reaping the benefits of the struggle against medieval autocracy, and had won their freedom from arbitrary taxation, arbitrary imprisonment and arbitrary legislation. But after the wars had done their destructive work the power of the Crown expanded to such an extent that it stifled individual liberty. 'The character of the monarchy from the time of Edward the Fourth to the time of Elizabeth remains something strange and isolated in our history. It is hard to connect the kingship of the old English, of the Norman, the Angevin, or the Plantagenet Kings, with the kingship of the House of York or the House of Tudor.'

Green's *Short History* was so influential, and its 'liberal' assumptions so in tune with the presuppositions of his age, that his interpretation gained general acceptance. All that later historians did was to modify some of the details, and in the textbooks, at any rate, 1485 rather than 1471 was taken as the date at which the 'New Monarchy' began. The advantage of making a break at 1485 was that it linked the arrival of a new dynasty on the English throne with the more widespread changes that were transforming European society from 'medieval' to 'modern'. Henry VII coincided with the Renaissance, and his son brought the Reformation to England. By these tokens they were obviously 'new monarchs', far removed in their methods and in their philosophy from their predecessors on the English throne.

The characteristics of this Tudor 'New Monarchy', as they were defined by later historians, were solvency, efficiency, autocratic centralisation, the development of the household at the expense of the older, more 'public' institutions, and the use of 'middle-class' men in place of feudal aristocrats. So far as Henry VII was concerned, his solvency is beyond question, but the other characteristics are not so easy to evaluate. It is true that Henry's government was efficient by the standards of its day, that it focused power upon the centre, and was autocratic to the extent that it stressed the royal authority and used a wide range of prerogative institutions and practices. It is also true that it worked through household institutions like the Chamber, rather than the Exchequer, and that its chief officials were drawn from the gentry rather than the nobility. In all these ways, then, Henry VII seems to conform to the pattern of a 'new monarch' and the battle of Bosworth can be held to signal the beginning of a new era in English history.

There is, however, another side to the picture. Solvency seems to have been characteristic only of Henry VII, not of the Tudors in general. As for efficiency, a great deal depends upon the meaning attached to this word. Henry VII's government was certainly more effective than Henry VI's but Henry VI was no more 'typically medieval' than Henry II or Edward I, whose effectiveness was never in doubt. Procrastination, deviousness and incapacity were not, in any case, unknown during the reign of Henry VII, and even in the financial sphere the absence of systematisation led to overlapping and duplication.

There are certainly centralising tendencies to be discerned in Henry VII's government, but what strikes a modern observer most about his administration is the way in which power was decentralised rather than concentrated. The facts of geography and poor communications were largely responsible for this, for the King simply had to leave a great deal of responsibility to the men on the spot. The Council could advise, encourage, warn and threaten, but in the last resort Henry was dependent upon the co-operation of the propertied section of society.

The same is true of the autocratic tendencies of the first Tudor. He may have wished to rule in the 'French manner', and he gave his court a degree of formality which emphasised the splendour of kingship. But Henry was never an absolute monarch. He was limited by custom and by law, and even had he wished to sweep away these barriers he could not have done so. He had no police force and no standing army. In time of danger even more than in time of peace he was dependent upon the support of the property-owners.

Henry's development of household administration and his reliance on 'middle class' men is often put forward as the most novel feature of his reign, but there was little that was 'new' about either of these. Medieval administration had never been confined to the Exchequer and Chancery, and during the reign of Edward III, for example, the Wardrobe had become in effect a national treasury. If there was nothing particularly new about Henry's use of the household departments nor was there in his reliance on the gentry rather than the aristocracy for his government. These were not 'middle class': indeed the term itself was unknown. They belonged to the upper section of English society, the political nation, and were new only in the sense that their families had not previously been prominent in central administration. They were advancing by a route which many had taken before them. Henry I, to mention only one of many examples, had been accused of raising men from the dust to serve him, and it may be accepted as a general rule that the 'new men' whom one King chose for his service founded aristocratic families which asserted a natural and exclusive right to advise his successors.

Henry did not begin his reign with a clean slate. The machinery of medieval government had survived the period of disorder and Henry was probably only too thankful to use it. The job of ruling late-medieval England was not an easy one, and institutions which had stood the test of time offered the best chance of doing it, for as a Venetian observer commented, 'If the King of England should propose to change any old-established rule, it would seem to every Englishman as if his life were taken away from him' (**72** p. 155). Henry did not have the doubtful advantage of knowing that the Middle Ages were over and that it was his task to lead his country into a new historical epoch. For him the problems of government were much as they had always been. So were the solutions. All that was needed was to make the existing system work properly.

In this Henry was not so different as is sometimes implied from his fellow monarchs, for in Europe as in England the evidence of the past was just as important as the evidence of the future. In France for example, although the Estates-General met only rarely and had lost its control over taxation, provincial assemblies continued their meetings and operated as an effective check upon the monarchy. The French king was theoretically free to raise as much money as he pleased, but in practice he had to accept the limitation imposed by the degree of public acceptance that he could command. He had royal officials working for him throughout France, but there were only some twelve thousand of them – far too few to hold down a population of about fifteen million. Nor, for that matter, could his standing army have done so, for it was limited in size and effectiveness and had to be supplemented in times of crisis by aristocratic retainers. France was in some ways a highly centralised monarchy, but the provinces, and especially those territories which had only recently come into possession of the crown, kept their separate privileges, customs, taxes and codes of law. An absolute ruler would have ridden roughshod over all these, but Charles VIII and Louis XII worked within the complex system they inherited and took it for granted. They would never have claimed, as Louis XIV is said to have done, that they alone embodied the state.

All European political communities in the early sixteenth century were the products of continuity as well as change, and this is why classifications such as 'New Monarchies' are only partially valid. One set of statements about what was 'typical' of the age can be paralleled by an opposite set. Henry VII's reign saw the triumph of the Crown, the subordination of parliament, the bringing to heel of the feudal nobility, the extension of the prerogative and the assertion of central control. But it also saw the survival of parliament and the increased use of statute, the continuance of the landowners as effective rulers of the localities, the reinvigoration of the ancient common law, and the preservation of privileges and franchises on a scale that no modern ruler would tolerate.

From the beginning of his reign until the end Henry deliberately exploited the rights of the Crown in order to make it once again rich and powerful. It may be that in his later years, when he was securely established on the throne, he acted in a more high-handed fashion and was less tender about the rights and liberties of his subjects. But it can be argued just as convincingly that the real change took place not in Henry's policy but in the attitude towards it of the property-owners. They had been prepared to pay a high price for good order after the breakdown of the late fifteenth century, but as they came to take more settled conditions for granted they resented the remorseless pressure of the royal administration and complained about its injustice [**doc. 5**]. There is no point in trying to distribute praise or blame. Henry VII, as King, was determined to rule and to find enough money to make his rule effective. If, in so doing, he and his servants sometimes acted tyrannically, it has to be borne in mind that failure to act effectively would have meant a return to anarchy. As for the property owners, by their determination to hold on to what was theirs they drove government to the very excesses of which they complained; but at the same time, and by the same determination, they preserved those legal and political liberties which in other countries were being eroded by the power of the state.

Henry VII cannot be neatly fitted into categories of 'new' or 'old', 'modern' or 'medieval'. He successfully founded a new dynasty but luck played a major part even in this: if Prince Henry had followed his brother Arthur to the grave, the peaceful accession of Henry's eldest daughter Margaret could not have been taken for granted, civil war might well have broken out again, and Henry VII would be remembered, if at all, simply as one more in the succession of late-medieval rulers who tried in vain to restore the strength of the monarchy and with it good order and government. No ruler, however successful, could hope to eradicate in the space of one reign the evils that afflicted contemporary England. Large bands of retainers were not unknown even in Elizabeth's day; 'bastard feudalism' was positively encouraged by Henry VIII when, for instance, he made the Russells the greatest family in the west country; and as for rioting and turbulence, these remained features of English life for several centuries after Henry VII's death.

Even in the more general context of the shift from 'medieval' to 'modern' Henry VII's reign marks no decisive break, for communities change gradually, and different aspects change at different rates. The supremacy of the Catholic Church, for example, which had been characteristic of the Middle Ages, survived Henry VII by less than one generation; villeinage lingered on into the seventeenth century, as did wardship; King's Bench, Common Pleas and the Court of the Exchequer kept their independent existence until well into the nineteenth century, while grand juries survived into the twentieth. No one would deny today that medieval England has long since vanished, but many of its institutions, in their outward form at any rate, are with us still. The monarchy survives, although its function has been radically altered; so does parliament and the common law. Even the formula used by Queen Elizabeth II to give the royal assent to statutes is the same as that used by Henry VII.

*[margin note: *** it was H.VIII who secured H.VII's name]*

The mixture of old and new in Henry's monarchy is symbolised by his tomb. In 1506, when he was considering the style in which he would be consigned to history, he chose as his sculptor Guido Mazzoni of Modena, who produced a design unlike anything that had ever been seen in England. In fact the tomb was not built until after Henry's death, and the work was carried out not by Mazzoni but by another Italian, Pietro Torrigiano of Florence. The sarcophagus itself, with the recumbent figures of Henry and his wife, Elizabeth of York, is Renaissance in inspiration and heralds the arrival in England of the new style that was transforming European art. Around the sarcophagus, however, is an exquisite bronze screen, the work of an English craftsman, Humphrey Walker, who designed it in the Perpendicular style which was England's unique contribution to Gothic art. To think of Henry VII as a Renaissance monarch confined within a late-medieval and specifically English setting is to come close to understanding the significance of his reign.

Part Four: Documents

A description of Henry VII

His body was slender but well built and strong; his height above the average. His appearance was remarkably attractive and his face was cheerful, especially when speaking; his eyes were small and blue, his teeth few, poor and blackish; his hair was thin and white; his complexion sallow. His spirit was distinguished, wise and prudent; his mind was brave and resolute, and never, even at moments of the greatest danger, deserted him. He had a most pertinacious memory. Withal he was not devoid of scholarship. In government he was shrewd and prudent, so that no one dared to get the better of him through deceit or guile. He was gracious and kind and was as attentive to his visitors as he was easy of access. His hospitality was splendidly generous; he was fond of having foreigners at his court and he freely conferred favours on them. But those of his subjects who were indebted to him and who did not pay him due honour or who were generous only with promises, he treated with harsh severity. He well knew how to maintain his royal majesty and all which appertains to kingship at every time and in every place. He was most fortunate in war, although he was constitutionally more inclined to peace than to war. He cherished justice above all things; as a result he vigorously punished violence, manslaughter and every other kind of wickedness whatsoever. Consequently he was greatly regretted on that account by all his subjects, who had been able to conduct their lives peaceably, far removed from the assaults and evil doing of scoundrels. He was the most ardent supporter of our faith, and daily participated with great piety in religious services. To those whom he considered to be worthy priests, he often secretly gave alms so that they should pray for his salvation. He was particularly fond of those Franciscan friars whom they call Observants, for whom he founded many convents, so that with his help their rule should continually flourish in his kingdom. But all these virtues were obscured latterly only by avarice, from which

... he suffered. This avarice is surely a bad enough vice in a private individual, whom it forever torments; in a monarch indeed it may be considered the worst vice, since it is harmful to everyone, and distorts those qualities of trustfulness, justice and integrity by which the state must be governed.

Vergil, (**17**), pp. 145–47.

document 2

Wardship

November 20, 1495: Grant to William Martyn, esquire, and William Twynyho, esquire, of the keeping of the lands late of John Trenchard, tenant in chief, and after the death of Margaret, widow of the said John, of the lands which she holds in dower; with the wardship and marriage of Thomas Trenchard, his son and heir.

October 3, 1487: Item. received of Richard Harp, receiver-general of the Duchy of Lancaster, for the ward and marriage of Humfrey Hill, £20.

February 26, 1503: Item. to Sir Richard Guilford in full payment of £200 for finding of the ward of Francis Cheyne, £30.

May 10, 1503: Item, received of Sir Reginald Bray for the ward and marriage of the two daughters of . . . Lovell of Sussex, £140.

Richardson, (**58**), pp. 166–67.

document 3

Dudley's account book September 1504–May 1508

Item. £20 in money for Robert Marshall to be receiver in Norfolk, Suffolk and Cambridgeshire, as Robert Strange was.

Item. delivered for the grant of the goods and chattels of one John Chauncy, forfeited by reason of an outlawry, £20 – viz. ten pounds in ready money and £10 by obligation.

Item. delivered the indenture between the king's grace and Lewes de la ffava concerning the lease of his royal ship called the Regent, and the customs outward and homeward of the said ship, for the which the said Lewes must pay to our said sovereign lord as in the same indenture appeareth for several causes the sum of five thousand and one hundred pounds.

Item. delivered for the Bishop of Lincoln for discharge of a fine of eight hundred marks for his mill and fishweirs upon the river Trent, three hundred pounds – viz. £100 in ready money, and £200 by obligation.

Richardson, (**58**), p. 156.

document 4

Bonds and recognisances

16 June 1505

[Recognisance] for £2,000 by Henry, Lord Clifford. Condition: Henry to keep the peace for himself and his servants, tenants and 'part takers', especially towards Roger Tempest of Broughton, and endeavour to bring before the King and his Council within 40 days such of his servants as were present at the late pulling down of Roger's place and house at Broughton.

Calendar of the Close Rolls, (**3**), vol. II, no. 499.

22 July 1506

Recognisance for £1,000 by Thomas West, Kt., Lord de la Warr, to Thomas Lovell and Richard Emson, Kts., and Edmund Dudley and Henry Wyat, esqs., to the King's use. Condition: payment of 100 marks a year at All Saints till he has given full satisfaction for 1,000 marks, and finding of sufficient surety or estate in land worth £120.

Calendar of the Close Rolls, (**3**), vol. II, no. 550.

24 December 1507

Indenture between the King and the same George, Lord Burgavenny: whereas George is indebted to the King in £100,000 or thereabouts for unlawful receivers done, retained and made by him in Kent contrary to certain laws and statutes, as was found by inquisitions certified into the King's Bench and adjudged after free confession by him in the said court in Michaelmas term last; and whereas for execution and levy of this debt, being clearly due both in law and conscience, the King may attach his body and keep him in prison and take all the issues of his lands till the whole sum be paid; the King is graciously contented, at his suit for avoiding the extremity of the law, to accept as parcel of the debt the sum of £5,000 payable over ten years at Candlemas and the Purification; for which payments, as well as the residue of the debt, George binds himself and his heirs.

Given 24 December, 23 Henry VII. Cancelled by warrant, 1 Henry VIII.

Calendar of the Close Rolls, (**3**), vol. II, no. 825.

document 5
The reaction against Empson and Dudley after the death of Henry VII

AN ACT FOR ADMITTANCE OF A TRAVERS AGAINST AN UNTRUE INQUISITION

Sheweth unto your discreet wisdoms that where divers and many untrue inquisitions by the procurement of Richard Empson, knight, and Edmond Dudley, have be had and take within this realm as well before commissioners assigned by letters patents of the late king, King Henry the vii[th], as before his exchetours, as well by virtue of writs of the said late king as by virtue of their office, by the which inquisitions sometime parcel of the said lands contained in the said inquisitions and sometime the hole lands there founden holden of the said late king *in capite*, where in truth the said lands contained in the said inquisitions nor no parcel of them was hold of the said late king *in capite* ne of any of his progenitors; to the which inquisitions the parties then grieved by the same could not nor might not take their travers to the same according to the law of this land, but were inforced and constrained to sue their livery of the same out of the hands of the said late king, whereby they were and be concluded to say but that the said lands be holden of the king in chief, to their great loss and hindrance, where in truth they were not holden of the said late king ne of any of his progenitors.

Wherefore be it enacted, ordained and established by the king our sovereign lord and the lords spiritual and temporal and the commons in this present parliament assembled, and by the authority of the same, that every person and persons having possession of the said lands contained in the same inquisitions or any part thereof may be admitted to have their travers to the said untrue inquisitions, notwithstanding any livery sued of the same in the time of the said late king, King Harry the vii[th].

1 Hen. VIII c. 12. From *The Statutes of the Realm*, vol. III, p. 7, London, 1817.

document 6

Decrees of the Council in Star Chamber

Sir Thomas Worthy and others are ordered to place Robert Inkarsall and Sibilla his wife in possession, and when they have been so placed to defend them by the authority of the lord king and in the name of his majesty, and to cause them to be defended to the utmost of their power against John Parker and William Parker and any others whomsoever. Because the said complainants were riotously and violently disseised by the defendants themselves. And they are ordered to answer when called on concerning punishment for rioting, and concerning damages, costs and the interest of the parties.

It is decreed that a letter be written by the lord king to the Earl of Surrey, that he himself place John Steward in possession or cause him to be placed in possession. And that when he has been placed in possession he cause him to be defended in that possession in the name of the lord king aforesaid in the case between John Steward and Lady Agnes Coneas, defendant.

Bayne, (**2**), pp. 25–7; modernised.

document 7

The 'Star Chamber' Act, 1487

The King our sovereign lord remembereth how by unlawful maintenances, giving of liveries, signs and tokens, and retainders by indenture, promises, oaths, writing or otherwise; embraceries of his subjects, untrue demeanings of sheriffs in making of panels and other untrue returns; by taking of money by juries, by great riots and unlawful assemblies; the policy and good rule of this realm is almost subdued. And for the non punishment of this inconvenience, and by occasion of the premises, nothing or little may be found by enquiry, whereby the laws of the land in execution may take little effect, to the increase of murders, robberies, perjuries and unsureties of all men living, and losses of their lands and goods, to the great displeasure of almighty God. Be it therefore ordained, for reformation of the premises, by the authority of this Parliament, that the Chancellor and Treasurer of England for the time being, and Keeper of the King's Privy Seal, or two of them, calling to him a bishop and a temporal lord of the King's most honourable Council, and the two Chief Justices of the King's Bench and Common Pleas for the time being, or other two justices in their absence, upon bill or information put to the said Chancellor, for the King or any other, against any person for any misbehaving afore rehearsed, have authority to call before them by writ or privy seal the said misdoers, and them and other[s] by their discretions, to whom the truth may be known, to examine; and such as they find therein defective, to punish them after their demerits, after the form and effect of statutes thereof made, in like manner and form as they should and ought to be punished if they were thereof convict after the due order of the law.

3 Hen. VII c. I. From *The Statutes of the Realm*, vol. II, pp. 509–10, London, 1817.

document 8

A case before the 1487 Tribunal

To the most reverend father in God, the Archbishop of Canterbury, Chancellor of England:

Showeth unto your good lordship James Hobart, attorney of the king our sovereign lord, that where one Robert Carvyle of Tilney in the shire of Norfolk, the xxix day of June in the second year of the reign of our sovereign lord the king that now is, was in his own proper soil in Tilney aforesaid, labouring in making hay; there came one Thomas Hunston with one of his servants whose name is unknown, in riotous wise, with force and arms – that is to say with long knives, a staff and a spear – and then and there riotously came out of the highway into the ground of the said Robert and ... made their assault and beat, wounded and maimed him, and left him almost dead, against the king's laws and peace.

And forasmuch as the said Robert, for the salvation of his life, defended himself with a scythe, which he then had in his hands to mow there with grass, and in the same defence happened with the same scythe to hurt the said Thomas, the same Thomas hath sued appeal of mayhem against the said Robert. In which appeal the said Robert pleaded to trial by jury; and thereupon xii partial men by special labour were empanelled, and by craft and subtle means, and also by great labour and embracery and by means of giving money unto them, were sworn to try the said matter. And by such unlawful occasions they passed judgment against the said Robert and taxed him with damages of C marks, against truth, reason and good conscience . . . By which occasion the said Robert is so impoverished that he is not of power to sue his lawful remedy, after the course of the common law.

May it please your good and gracious lordship, in eschewing of such open and abominable perjury in time to come, to direct several writs of subpoena as well to the said Thomas as to the said xii men, commanding them by the same to appear before your lordship, my Lord Treasurer and my Lord Privy Seal, or two of you and others, at a certain day, after the effect and form of a statute made in the last Parliament of our said sovereign lord [**doc. 7**], and thereupon to proceed and do in that behalf as well for punishing the said Thomas for the said riot and other misbehavings as all the said persons which so passed judgment, as shall accord with reason and your good discretions and with the force and effect of the said statute and other statutes afore time made. And our blessed Saviour preserve your good and gracious lordship.

Bayne, (**2**), pp. 62–3; modernised.

document 9

JPs to check jury panels, 1495

AN ACT AGAINST PERJURY, UNLAWFUL MAINTENANCE AND CORRUPTION IN OFFICERS

The king our sovereign lord, well understanding the heinous and detestable perjuries daily committed within this realm in inquests and juries . . . to the high displeasure of almighty God and letting [hindering] of administration and justice; the which perjury groweth by unlawful retainders, maintenance, embracing* . . . as well of the sheriffs as of other officers, notwithstanding any laws before this time made for the punishment of such offenders; Wherefore the

---

* Maintenance: the use of unlawful means – violence, threats, bribery, etc. – to support a person involved in a law suit.
Embracing: the corrupting of juries.

king our said sovereign lord . . . willeth and commandeth that all the said laws be duly put in execution.

And it is ordained by the said authority [of Parliament] that the justices of the peace within this realm, in any inquests of office before them or any of them to be taken, admit nor take any panel of such inquests to be returned afore them, but if the same panel be first seen before them, and they to reform it by their discretion if cause be.

11 Hen. VII c. 25. From *The Statutes of the Realm*, vol. II, p. 589, London, 1817.

document 10

An indenture of Retainder

25th April 1481

This indenture made the xxv day of April the xxi year of the reign of King Edward the IV between William Hastings, knight, Lord Hastings, on the one part, and Ralph Longford, esquire, on the other part, witnesseth that the said Ralph agreeth, granteth, and by these present indentures bindeth him to the said lord to be his retained servant during his life, and to him to do faithful and true service, and the part of the same lord take against all men in peace and war with as many persons defensibly arrayed as the same Ralph can or may make at all times that the said lord will command him, at the said lord's costs and charges, saving the allegiance which the same Ralph oweth to the king our sovereign lord and to the prince. And the said lord granteth to the said Ralph to be his good and favourable lord and him aid and support in his right according to the law. In witness hereof the foresaid parties to these present indentures have interchangeably set their seals and signs manual the day and year aforesaid.

Dunham, (**36**), p. 132.

document 11

Form of a licence to retain

Henry, by the grace of God, King of England and of France and lord of Ireland – greeting. . . . WE . . . by the advice of our Council, intending to provide a good, substantial and competent number of captains and able men of our subjects to be in a readiness to serve us at our pleasure when the case shall require, and trusting in your faith and truth, will and desire you, and . . . by these presents give unto your full power and authority from henceforth during our pleasure to take, appoint and retain by indenture or covenant in form or manner as hereafter ensueth, and none otherwise, such persons our subjects as by your discretion shall be thought and seemeth to you to be able men to do us service in the war in your company under you and at your leading at all times and places and as often as it shall please us to command or assign you, to the number of — persons, whose names be contained in a certificate by you made in a bill of parchment indented betwixt us and you and interchangeably signed by us and subscribed with your hand and to our secretary delivered. . . . PROVIDED always that you retain not above the said number which you shall indent for in form and manner hereafter ensuing. PROVIDED also the same able persons shall not be chosen, taken nor retained but only of your own tenants or of the inhabitants within any office that you have of our grant . . . And these our present letters shall be unto you, and all and every the persons by you to be retained in form above specified and indented for with us, and such other as you shall retain in the place of any of them died, avoided or discharged as above is specified, sufficient discharge in this behalf at all times hereafter, any act, statute, prohibition or other ordinance in the time of us or any of our noble progenitors or predecessors, by authority of parliament or otherwise, heretofore made, enacted, passed or ordained to the contrary notwithstanding. PROVIDED always that you, under colour hereof or by virtue of these our letters of placard, retain no more in number by word, promise or otherwise than is contained in your said certificate indented and indented for with us as above, under the pains specified in our statutes made and ordained in that behalf.

Dunham, (**36**) pp. 148–50.

document 12

The Yeomen of the Guard

Henry, moreover, was the first English king to appoint retainers, to the number of about two hundred, to be a bodyguard: these he incorporated in his household so that they should never leave his side; in this he imitated the French kings so that he might thereafter be better protected from treachery.

Vergil, (**17**), p. 7.

document 13

The Speaker's petition for privilege, 1485

That everything to be proffered and declared in the aforesaid parliament in the name of the said Commons, he might proffer and declare under such protestation that if he should have declared anything enjoined on him by his fellows otherwise than they had agreed, or with any addition or omission, that then what he had so declared might be corrected and emended by his fellows; and that his protestation to this effect might be entered on the roll of the aforesaid parliament.

From *Rotuli Parliamentorum*, vol. VI, p. 268, London, 1783.

document 14

The grant of tunnage and poundage, 1485

To the worship of God. We, your poor Commons, by your high commandment come to this your present Parliament assembled, grant by this present indenture to you, our sovereign lord, for the defence of this your said realm, and in especial for the safeguard and keeping of the sea, a subsidy called Tonnage, to be taken in manner and form following: that is to say, iiis. of every Ton of wine coming into this your said realm, and of every Ton of sweet wine coming into the same your realm; by every merchant alien, as well by the merchants of Hansa and of Almain as of any other merchant aliens, iiis. over the said iiis. afore granted: to have and to perceive yearly the said subsidy, from the first day of this present Parliament, for term of your life natural. And over that, we your said Commons, by the assent aforesaid, grant to you, our said sovereign lord, for the safeguard and keeping of the sea, another subsidy called Poundage.

From *Rotuli Parliamentorum*, vol. VI, pp. 268–69, London, 1783.

document 15

A forced loan, 1486

The king sent my lord Treasurer with master Bray and other honourable personages unto the mayor, requiring him and his citizens
of a loan of vi thousand marks, wherefore the mayor assembled his
brethren and the Common Council upon the Tuesday following.
By whose authority was then granted to the king a loan of £2,000,
the which for him was shortly levied after, and this was assessed
by the fellowships and not by the wards, for the more ease of the
poor people. Of the which loan the fellowships of mercers, grocers
and drapers lent £ixCxxxvii. vis. The which loan was justly repaid
in the year following.

Fabian, (**9**), p. 240.

document 16

Benevolences

The king – lest the poorer sort should be burdened with the charge
of paying the troops for the war – levied money from the rich only,
each contributing to the pay of the troops according to his means.
Since it was the responsibility of each individual to contribute a
great or a small sum, this type of tax was called a 'benevolence'.
Henry in this copied King Edward IV, who first . . . raised money
from the people under the name of loving kindness. In this process
it could be perceived precisely how much each person cherished the
king – something which it had not before been possible to observe –
for the man who paid most was presumed to be most dutiful;
many none the less secretly grudged their contribution, so that this
method of taxation might more appropriately be termed a 'mal-
evolence' rather than a 'benevolence'. However, since no one would
have it said he was less dutiful, all competed to pay the required
money.

Vergil, (**17**), p. 49.

document 17

Parliamentary supply, 1491

To the worship of God: we your Commons, by your high commandment come to this your present Parliament for the shires, cit-

ies and burghs of this your noble realm, calling to our remembrance the great continued zeal, love and tenderness which your royal person hath to defend this your realm and all your subjects of the same . . . and that ye verily intending, as we understand . . . in your most noble person to invade upon your and our ancient enemies with an army royal . . . to subdue by the might of God your and our said ancient enemies to the weal of you and prosperity of this your realm; so that your said highness might have therein of us your said Commons loving assistance; for the which we, your said Commons, by the assent of the Lords spiritual and temporal in this your present Parliament assembled, grant by this present indenture to you our sovereign liege lord, for the necessary defence of this your said realm, and us your said true subjects of the same, ii whole xv^{mes} and x^{mes} to be had, paid, taken and levied of the moveable goods, chattels and other things usually to such xv^{mes} and x^{mes} contributory and chargeable within the shires, cities, burghs and towns and other places of this your said realm, in manner and form aforetime used.

7 Hen. VII c. 11. From *The Statutes of the Realm*, vol. II, p. 555, London, 1817.

document 18

The Royal Title, 1485

To the pleasure of almighty God, the wealth, prosperity and surety of this realm of England, to the singular comfort of all the king's subjects of the same, and in avoiding of all ambiguities and questions, be it ordained, established and enacted by authority of this present Parliament that the inheritance of the crowns of the realms of England and of France, with all the preeminence and dignity royal to the same pertaining, and all other seignories to the king belonging beyond the sea, with the appurtenances thereto in any wise due or pertaining, be, rest, remain and abide in the most royal person of our now sovereign lord King Harry the VIIth and in the heirs of his body lawfully coming, perpetually with the grace of God so to endure, and in none other.

From *The Statutes of the Realm*, vol. II, p. 499, London, 1817.

document 19

An Act of attainder, 1491

Forasmuch as Sir Robert Chamberleyn, late of Barking in the shire of Essex, knight, and Richard White, late of Thorpe beside Billingforde in the shire of Norfolk, gentleman, the xxiii day of August, and the said Sir Robert the xvii day of January the vi[th] year of the reign of our sovereign lord the king that now is, at Barking aforesaid traitorously imagined and compassed the death and destruction of our said sovereign lord, and also the subversion of all this realm, then and there traitorously levied war against our said sovereign lord and adhered them traitorously to Charles the French king, ancient enemy to our said sovereign lord and this realm, against their duty and liegance; Be it therefore ordained and enacted by authority of this present Parliament that the said Robert and Richard stand and be attainted of high treason, and forfeit all manors, lands, tenements, rents, reversions and all other hereditaments that they or either of them or any other to their use or to the use of either of them had at any of the said days, of estate of fee simple or fee tail in England or Wales.

From *The Statutes of the Realm*, vol. II, p. 566, London, 1817.

document 20

Auto da fé

Upon the xxviii day of April was an old cankered heretic, weakminded for age, named Joan Boughton, widow, and mother unto the wife of Sir John Young – which daughter, as some reported, had a great smell of an heretic after the mother – burnt in Smithfield. This woman was iiii score years of age or more, and held viii opinions of heresy which I pass over, for the hearing of them is neither pleasant nor fruitful. She was a disciple of Wyclif, whom she accounted for a saint, and held so fast and firmly viii of his xii opinions that all the doctors of London could not turn her from one of them. When it was told to her that she should be burnt for her obstinacy and false belief, she set nought at their words but defied them, for she said she was so beloved with God and His holy angels that all the fire in London should not hurt her. But on the morrow a bundle of faggots and a few reeds consumed her in a little while; and while she might cry she spake often of God and Our Lady, but no man could cause her to name Jesus, and so she died. But it appeared that she left some of her disciples behind her, for the night following, the more part of the ashes of that fire that she was burnt in were had away and kept for a precious relic in an earthen pot.

Fabian, (**9**), p. 252.

document 21

New found men, 1502

This year were brought unto the king iii men taken in the New Found Isle land. These were clothed in beasts' skins and ate raw flesh and spake such speech that no man could understand them, and in their demeanour like to brute beasts, whom the king kept a time after. Of the which, upon ii years passed after, I saw ii of them apparelled after Englishmen, in Westminster Palace, which at that time I could not discern from Englishmen till I was learned what men they were. But as for speech, I heard none of them utter one word.

Fabian, (**9**), p. 320.

document 22

A Navigation Act, 1485

AN ACT AGAINST BRINGING IN OF GASCON WINE EXCEPT IN ENGLISH, IRISH OR WELSHMEN'S SHIPS

To the right wise and discreet Commons in this present Parliament assembled. Please it your great wisdoms to call to your remembrance of the great minishing and decay that hath been now of late time of the navy within this realm of England, and idleness of the mariners within the same, by the which this noble realm within short process of time, without reformation be had therein, shall not be of ability and power to defend itself. Wherefore please it your great wisdoms to pray the king our sovereign lord that he, by the advice of his lords spiritual and temporal, and of you his Commons, in this present Parliament assembled, and by authority of the same, it be enacted, ordained and established that no manner person of what degree or condition that he be of, buy nor sell within this said realm, Ireland, Wales, Calais or the marches thereof, or Berwick, from the feast of Michaelmas next now coming, any manner wines of the growing of the duchy of Guienne or of Gascony, but such as shall be adventured and brought in an English, Irish or Welsh-man's ship or ships, and the mariners of the same English, Irish or Welshman for the more part, or men of Calais or of the marches of the same; and that upon pain of forfeiture of the same wines so bought or sold contrary to this act, the one half of that forfeiture to be to the king's grace and that other half to the finder of the forfeiture.

1 Hen. VII c. 8. From *The Statutes of the Realm*, vol. II, p. 502, London, 1817.

Chronological Summary

1457 Jan 28. Henry born at Pembroke Castle.

1461 Edward IV defeats and deposes Henry VI and claims throne.

1470 Restoration of Henry VI.

1471 Edward IV recovers throne.
Death of Henry VI and Edward, Prince of Wales.
Henry goes into exile in Brittany.

1477 Marriage of Ferdinand, King of Aragon, to Isabella, Queen of Castile.
Death of Charles the Bold, Duke of Burgundy.

1483 Death of Edward IV.
Accession of Richard III.
Probable death of Edward V and his brother Richard, Duke of York.
Buckingham's Rebellion.
Death of Louis XI of France: accession of Charles VIII·

1484 Henry leaves Brittany for France.

1485 August: Henry lands in Milford Haven. Battle of Bosworth.
September: Henry enters London.
October: Coronation.
November: Meeting of first parliament.

1486 Anglo-French commercial treaty.
January: Henry marries Elizabeth of York.
March: Lovell's conspiracy.
September: Birth of Prince Arthur.

1487 France invades Brittany.
Bartholomew Diaz rounds Cape of Good Hope.
May: Simnel crowned in Dublin.
June: Battle of Stoke.
November: Henry's second parliament.

1488 Defeat of Breton army by French.
Death of Duke of Brittany: accession of Anne as duchess.
June: Death of James III of Scotland: accession of James IV.

3-year truce between England and Scotland.
July: Anglo-French truce renewed.

1489 Anglo-Portuguese treaty of friendship renewed.
January: Henry's third parliament.
February: Treaty of Redon between England and Brittany.
March: Treaty of Medina del Campo between England and Spain.
April: Assassination of Earl of Northumberland.

1490 Renewal of Anglo-Danish commerical treaty.
Commercial treaty with Florence.

1491 Henry sends army to Ireland.
October: Henry's fourth parliament.
December: Charles VIII marries Anne of Brittany.

1492 Spain conquers Granada.
Columbus discovers America.
October: Henry lands in France.
November: Treaty of Etaples between England and France.

1493 Death of Emperor Frederick III: accession of Maximilian I.
Philip of Burgundy takes over effective rule of Netherlands.
Henry imposes embargo on Anglo-Flemish trade.
Attack on the Steelyard.
7-year truce between England and Scotland.

1494 September: Charles VIII invades Italy.
December: Irish parliament passes Poynings' Law.

1495 February: Sir William Stanley executed.
Charles VIII enters Naples.
March: Formation of Holy League.
July: Warbeck lands troops at Deal.
October: Henry's fifth parliament.
November: Charles VIII leaves Italy.

1496 February: *Magnus Intercursus*.
July: Henry joins Holy League.
September: James IV of Scotland and Warbeck invade England.
October: Philip of Burgundy marries Joanna.

1497 Anglo-French treaty of commerce.
Cabot discovers Newfoundland.
Vasco da Gama rounds Cape.
January: Henry's sixth parliament.
June: Defeat of Cornish rebels.
September: Warbeck lands in Cornwall, and is captured.

Truce of Ayton between England and Scotland.
December: Destruction by fire of Henry's palace at Sheen.

1498 Vasco da Gama reaches India.
Columbus discovers South American mainland.
April: Death of Charles VIII of France: accession of Louis XII.

1499 Commercial treaty with Riga.
September: Louis XII occupies Milan.
November: Execution of Warbeck and Warwick.

1500 Henry goes to Calais for meeting with Philip of Burgundy.

1501 Flight of Edmund de la Pole, Earl of Suffolk.
November: Marriage of Prince Arthur and Catherine of Aragon.

1502 Anglo-Scottish treaty of peace and alliance.
April: death of Prince Arthur.
July: Treaty between Henry and Maximilian.

1503 Spanish drive out French from Naples.
Work starts on Henry VII Chapel in Westminster Abbey.
February: Death of Elizabeth of York.
August: Marriage of James IV of Scotland to Princess Margaret.

1504 France abandons claims on Naples.
Henry imposes embargo on Anglo-Flemish trade.
January: Henry's seventh and last parliament.
November: Death of Isabella, Queen of Castile.

1506 January: Philip and Joanna in England.
 Malus Intercursus.
 Surrender of Earl of Suffolk arranged.
September: Death of Philip.

1508 December: League of Cambrai.
Proxy marriage of future Charles V to Princess Mary.

1509 April 21. Death of Henry VII at Richmond Palace.

LANCASTRIANS, YORKISTS AND TUDORS

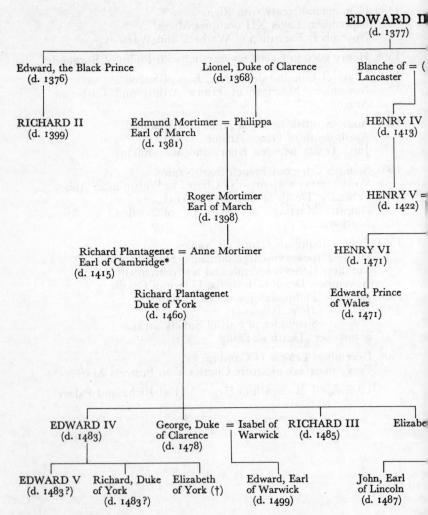

EDWARD I‍I
(d. 1377)

Edward, the Black Prince
(d. 1376)

Lionel, Duke of Clarence
(d. 1368)

Blanche of = (
Lancaster

RICHARD II
(d. 1399)

Edmund Mortimer = Philippa
Earl of March
(d. 1381)

HENRY IV
(d. 1413)

Roger Mortimer
Earl of March
(d. 1398)

HENRY V =
(d. 1422)

Richard Plantagenet = Anne Mortimer
Earl of Cambridge*
(d. 1415)

HENRY VI
(d. 1471)

Richard Plantagenet
Duke of York
(d. 1460)

Edward, Prince
of Wales
(d. 1471)

EDWARD IV
(d. 1483)

George, Duke = Isabel of
of Clarence   Warwick
(d. 1478)

RICHARD III
(d. 1485)

Elizabe

EDWARD V
(d. 1483?)

Richard, Duke
of York
(d. 1483?)

Elizabeth
of York (†)

Edward, Earl
of Warwick
(d. 1499)

John, Earl
of Lincoln
(d. 1487)

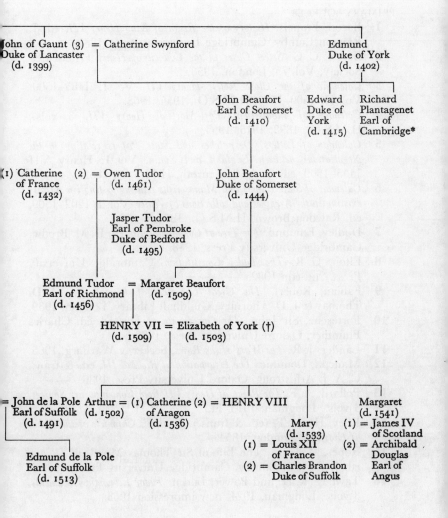

John of Gaunt (3) = Catherine Swynford
Duke of Lancaster
(d. 1399)

Edmund
Duke of York
(d. 1402)

John Beaufort
Earl of Somerset
(d. 1410)

Edward
Duke of
York
(d. 1415)

Richard
Plantagenet
Earl of
Cambridge*

(1) Catherine (2) = Owen Tudor
of France   (d. 1461)
(d. 1432)

John Beaufort
Duke of Somerset
(d. 1444)

Jasper Tudor
Earl of Pembroke
Duke of Bedford
(d. 1495)

Edmund Tudor = Margaret Beaufort
Earl of Richmond   (d. 1509)
(d. 1456)

HENRY VII = Elizabeth of York (†)
(d. 1509)   (d. 1503)

= John de la Pole Arthur = (1) Catherine (2) = HENRY VIII
Earl of Suffolk   (d. 1502) of Aragon
(d. 1491)   (d. 1536)

Margaret
(d. 1541)
(1) = James IV
      of Scotland
(2) = Archibald
      Douglas
      Earl of
      Angus

Mary
(d. 1533)
(1) = Louis XII
      of France
(2) = Charles Brandon
      Duke of Suffolk

Edmund de la Pole
Earl of Suffolk
(d. 1513)

Bibliography

PRIMARY SOURCES

1 Bacon, Francis. *History of the Reign of King Henry VII*, ed. J. Rawson Lumby, Cambridge University Press, 1881.

2 Bayne, C. G. *Select Cases in the Council of Henry VII*, Selden Society, Vol. 75, London, 1958.

3 *Calendar of the Close Rolls. Henry VII*, Vol. I, 1485–1500; Vol. II, 1500–1509, H.M.S.O., 1955, 1963.

4 *Calendar of Inquisitions Post-Mortem. Henry VII*, 3 vols., H.M.S.O., 1898, 1915, 1955.

5 *Calendar of Letters, Despatches and State Papers relating to the Negotiations between England and Spain*, Vol. I, Henry VII 1485–1509, ed. G. A. Bergenroth, H.M.S.O., 1862.

6 *Calendar of State Papers and Manuscripts relating to English Affairs existing in the Archives and collections of Venice*. Vol. I. 1202–1509, ed. Rawdon Brown, H.M.S.O., 1864.

7 Dudley, Edmund. *The Tree of Commonwealth*, ed. D. M. Brodie, Cambridge University Press, 1948.

8 Elton, G. R. *The Tudor Constitution*, Cambridge University Press, 2nd edn 1982.

9 Fabian, Robert. *The Great Chronicle of London*, ed. A. D. Thomas & I. D. Thornley, Guildhall Library, London, 1939.

10 Fortescue, Sir John. *The Governance of England*, ed. Charles Plummer, Oxford University Press, 1885.

11 Lander, J. R. *The Wars of the Roses*, Secker & Warburg, 1965.

12 Mancini, Dominic. *The Usurpation of Richard III*, ed. & trans. C. A. J. Armstrong, Oxford University Press, 1936.

13 Pollard, A. F. *The Reign of Henry VII from Contemporary Sources*, 3 vols., Longman, 1913–14.

14 Riley, Henry T. (ed. & trans.). *Ingulph's Chronicle of the Abbey of Croyland*, London, 1854.

15 Roper, William. 'The Life of Sir Thomas More', in *Utopia*, ed. J. Rawson Lumby, Cambridge University Press, 1879.

16 Tawney, R. H. and Power, Eileen. *Tudor Economic Documents*, 3 vols., Longman, 1924, new impression 1963.

17 Vergil, Polydore. *The Anglica Historia 1485–1537*, ed. & trans. Denys Hay, Camden Series Vol. 74, Royal Historical Society, London, 1950.

18 Wedgwood, J. C. (ed.) *History of Parliament 1439–1509*, H.M.S.O., 1938.

19 Williams, C. H. (ed.) *English Historical Documents*, Vol. V 1485–1558, Eyre & Spottiswoode, 1967.

BOOKS, DISSERTATIONS AND ESSAYS

20 Baker, J. H. Introduction to *The Reports of Sir John Spelman*, Vol. II, Selden Society, London, 1978.

21 Batho, Gordon. 'The Golden Age of the Crown Estate, 1461–1509' in Thirsk, 62.

22 Beresford, M. W. *Deserted Medieval Villages*, Lutterworth Press, 1971.

23 Beresford, M. W. and St Joseph, J. K. *Medieval England. An Aerial Survey*, 2nd edn., Cambridge University Press, 1979.

24 Blatcher, Margaret. *The Court of King's Bench 1450–1550*, Athlone Press, 1978.

25 Bowker, Margaret. *The Secular Clergy in the Diocese of Lincoln 1495–1520*, Cambridge University Press, 1968.

26 Bradshaw, Brendan. *The Irish Constitutional Revolution of the Sixteenth Century*, Cambridge University Press, 1979.

27 Brooks, F. W. *The Council of the North*, Historical Association pamphlet G. 25., 1966.

28 Challis, C. E. *The Tudor Coinage*, Manchester University Press, 1978.

29 Chrimes, S. B. *Henry VII*, Eyre Methuen, 1972.

30 Chrimes, S. B., Ross, C. D. and Griffiths, R. A. *Fifteenth-Century England 1399–1509*, Manchester University Press, 1972.

31 Clark, Peter and Slack, Paul. *English Towns in Transition 1500–1700*, Oxford University Press, 1976.

32 Coleman, D. C. *The Economy of England 1450–1750*, Oxford University Press, 1977.

33 Cook, David. *Lancastrians and Yorkists: The Wars of the Roses*, Longman, 1984.

34 Cross, Claire. *Church and People 1450–1660*, Fontana, 1976.

35 Dunlop, Ian. *Palaces and Progresses of Elizabeth I*, Cape, 1962.

36 Dunham, W. H. Jnr. *Lord Hastings' Indentured Retainers 1461–1483; The Lawfulness of Livery and Retaining under the Yorkists and Tudors*, Transactions of the Connecticut Academy of Arts and Sciences, Vol. 39, Yale University Press, 1955.

37 Elton. G. R. *Studies in Tudor and Stuart Politics and Government,* Cambridge University Press, 1974.

38 Gillingham, John. *The Wars of the Roses,* Weidenfeld & Nicolson, 1981.

39 Goodman, Anthony. *The Wars of the Roses: Military Activity and English Society 1452–97,* Routledge & Kegan Paul, 1981.

40 Fletcher, Anthony. *Tudor Rebellions,* 3rd edn, Longman, 1983.

41 Guth, DeLoyd-J. 'Enforcing late medieval Law: patterns in litigation during Henry VII's reign', in Baker, J. H. (ed), *Legal Records and the Historian,* Royal Historical Society, London, 1978.

42 Guy, J. A. *The Cardinal's Court; the Impact of Thomas Wolsey in Star Chamber,* Harvester Press, 1977.

43 Hay, Denys. 'The early Renaissance in England' in Carter, C. H. (ed.), *From the Renaissance to the Counter-Reformation,* Cape, 1966.

44 Heath, Peter. *The English Parish Clergy on the Eve of the Reformation,* Routledge & Kegan Paul, 1969.

45 Heinze, R. W. *The Proclamations of the Tudor Kings,* Cambridge University Press, 1976.

46 Hexter, J. H. 'The myth of the middle class in Tudor England' in Hexter, J. H., *Reappraisals in History,* Longman, 1961.

47 Hoskins, W. G. *The Making of the English Landscape,* Hodder and Stoughton, 1955.

48 James, M. E. *A Tudor Magnate and the Tudor State: Henry, Fifth Earl of Northumberland,* Borthwick Papers No. 30, St Anthony's Press, York, 1966.

49 Kipling, Gordon. 'Henry VII and the origins of Tudor Patronage' in Lytle, G. F. and Orgel, S. (eds.), *Patronage in the Renaissance,* Princeton University Press, 1981.

50 Knowles, Dom David. *The Religious Orders in England, Vol. III, The Tudor Age,* Cambridge University Press, 1961.

51 Lander, J. R. *Crown and Nobility 1450–1509,* Edward Arnold, 1976.

52 Lander, J. R. *Government and Community. England 1450–1509,* Edward Arnold, 1980.

53 Morris, Christopher. *The Tudors,* Batsford, 1955.

54 Myers, A. R. 'Parliament 1422–1509' in Davies, R. G. and Denton, J. H. (eds.), *The English Parliament in the Middle Ages: A Tribute to J. S. Roskell,* Manchester University Press, 1981.

55 Pronay, Nicholas. 'The Chancellor, the Chancery, and the Council at the end of the fifteenth century' in Hearder, H.

and Lyon, H. R. (eds.), *British Government and Administration*, University of Wales Press, 1974.

56 Ramsay, G. D. *English Overseas Trade during the Centuries of Emergence*, Macmillan, 1957.

57 Reynolds, Susan. *An Introduction to the History of English Medieval Towns*, Clarendon Press, Oxford, 1977.

58 Richardson, W. C. *Tudor Chamber Administration 1485–1547*, Louisiana State University Press, 1952.

59 Ross, Charles. *Edward IV*, Eyre Methuen, 1974.

60 Ross, Charles. *Richard III*, Eyre Methuen, 1981.

61 Starkey, David. 'The King's Privy Chamber', Cambridge University Ph.D. thesis. 1973.

62 Thirsk, Joan (ed.). *The Agrarian History of England and Wales*, Vol. IV, 1500–1640, Cambridge University Press, 1967.

63 Wernham, R. B. *Before the Armada: the Growth of English Foreign Policy 1485–1588*, Cape, 1966.

64 Wilkie, W. E. *The Cardinal Protectors of England: Rome and the Tudors before the Reformation*, Cambridge University Press 1974.

65 Williams, Penry. *The Council in the Marches of Wales under Elizabeth I*, University of Wales Press, 1958.

66 Williams, Penry. *The Tudor Regime*, Clarendon Press, Oxford, 1979.

67 Wolffe, B. P. *Yorkist and Early Tudor Government 1461–1509*. Historical Association 'Aids for Teachers' series no. 12, 1966.

68 Wolffe, B. P. *The Crown Lands 1461 to 1536. An Aspect of Yorkist and Early Tudor Government*, Allen & Unwin, 1970.

69 Wolffe, B. P. *The Royal Demesne in English History. The Crown Estate in the Governance of the Realm from the Conquest to 1509*, Allen & Unwin, 1971.

ARTICLES

70 Blanchard, Ian. 'Population change, enclosure, and the early Tudor economy', *Econ. History Review*, 23 (1970).

71 Bridbury, A. R. 'Sixteenth-century farming', *Econ. History Review*, 27 (1974).

72 Brodie, D. M. 'Edmund Dudley, minister of Henry VII'. *Transacts. Royal Historical Soc.* (4th ser.), 15 (1932).

73 Cameron, A. 'A Nottinghamshire quarrel in the reign of Henry VII', *Bulletin Instit. Historical Research*, 45 (1972).

74 Cameron, A. 'The giving of livery and retaining in Henry VII's reign', *Renaissance & Modern Studies*, 18 (1974).

75 Chrimes, S. B. 'The reign of Henry VII. Some recent contributions', *Welsh Hist. Review*, 10 (1981).

76 Cooper, J. P. 'Henry VII's last years reconsidered', *Historical Jnl*, 2 (1959).

77 Dyer, Christoper. 'Deserted medieval villages in the West Midlands', *Econ. History Review*, 35 (1982).

78 Ellis, Steven G. 'Tudor policy and the Kildare Ascendancy in the Lordship of Ireland 1496–1534', *Irish Historical Review*, 20 (1977).

79 Elton, G. R. 'Henry VII. Repacity and remorse in **37** vol. I.

80 Elton, G. R. 'Henry VII. A restatement' in **37**, vol. I.

81 Elton, G. R. 'Why the history of the early Tudor Council remains unwritten' in **37**, vol. I.

82 Elton, G. R. '"The body of the whole realm", Parliament and representation in medieval and Tudor England' in **37**, vol. II.

83 Elton. G. R. 'The rolls of Parliament 1449–1547'. *Historical Jnl*, 22 (1979).

84 Gottfried, R. S. 'Population, plague, and the sweating sickness: demographic movements in late fifteenth-century England', *Jnl Brit. Studies*, 17 (1977).

85 Guy, J. A. 'A Conciliar Court of Audit at work in the last months of the reign of Henry VII', *Bulletin Instit. Historical Research*, 49 (1976).

86 Harper-Bill, Christopher. 'Archbishop John Morton and the Province of Canterbury 1486–1500'. *Jnl Eccles. Hist.*, 29 (1978).

87 Harriss, G. L. 'Aids, loans and benevolences', *Historical Jnl*, 6 (1963).

88 Hay, Denys. 'Late medieval – early modern', *Bulletin Instit. Historical Research*, 24 (1951).

89 Hicks, M. A. 'Dynastic change and northern society: the career of the fourth Earl of Northumberland 1470–89'. *Northern Hist.*, 14 (1978).

90 Hoskins, W. G. 'Harvest fluctuations and English economic history 1480–1619', *Agric. Hist. Review*, 12 (1964).

91 Ives, E. W. 'The common lawyers in pre-reformation England'. *Transacts. Royal Historical Soc.* (5th ser.), 18 (1968).

92 Lander, J. R. 'Attainder and forfeiture 1453–1509' in **51**.

93 Lander, J. R. 'Edward IV. The modern legend and a revision' in **51**.

94 Lander, J. R. 'The Yorkist Council and administration 1461–85' in **51**.

95 Lander, J. R. 'Council, administration, and Councillors 1461–85' in **51**.

96 Lander, J. R. 'Bonds, coercion and fear' in **51**.

97 Palliser, D. M. 'A crisis in English towns? The case of York 1460–1640', *Northern Hist.*, 14 (1978).

98 Ramsey, Peter. 'Overseas trade in the reign of Henry VII: the evidence of the Customs accounts', *Econ. History Review*, 6 (1963).

99 Richardson, W. C. 'The surveyor of the King's prerogative', *Eng. Historical Review*, 56 (1941).

100 Richmond, C. F. 'English naval power in the fifteenth century', *History*, 52 (1967).

101 Somerville, R. 'Henry VII's Council Learned in the Law', *Eng. Historical Review*, 54 (1939).

102 Thomson, J. A. F. 'Piety and charity in late-medieval London', *Jnl. Eccles. Hist.*, 16 (1965).

103 Weiss, Michael. 'A power in the north? The Percies in the fifteenth century', *Northern Hist.*, 19 (1976).

104 Wolffe, B. P. 'The management of English royal estates under the Yorkist kings', *Eng. Historical Review*, 71 (1956).

105 Wolffe, B. P 'Henry VII's land revenues and Chamber finance', *Eng. Historical Review*, 79 (1964).

106 Horowitz, M. R. 'Richard Empson, minister of Henry VII', *Bulletin Instit. Historical Research*, 55 (1982).

107 Colvin, Howard (ed.), The History of the King's Works, Vol. III, 1485–1660 Part I; Vol. IV, 1485–1660 Part II, HMSO, 1975, 1982.

108 Kermode, Jennifer I. 'Urban decline? The flight from office in late medieval York', *Econ. History Review*, 35 (1982).

Index